Ed Galloway's
Totem Pole Park

The Story Behind One of the Greatest Folk-Art Attractions on America's
Mother Road, Route 66.

By John Wooley

This book was commissioned by the Rogers County Historical Society in order to document for posterity the life and accomplishments of the interesting, industrious, and exceptionally talented man who built the Totem Pole Park, as well as to acknowledge with gratitude those who have worked so tirelessly to restore and preserve it for future generations.

Rogers County Historical Society
P.O. Box 774 Claremore, Ok 74018
http://www.rchs1.org/

Totem Pole Park can be located at:
36°26'15.29" N   95°26'53.53" W
21300 E Highway 28A
Chelsea Oklahoma,
United States

Layout and design by David Anderson
Director, Totem Pole Park.

Available from Amazon.com and other retail outlets
Available on Kindle and other devices

ISBN:1502348349
ISBN-13:9781502348340

DEDICATION

To the Galloway family, who made sure Ed Galloway's creations would live on to attract and fascinate future generations by donating the park and much of Mr. Galloway's other work to the Rogers County Historical Society.

To those special groups and people responsible for the resurrection and management of Totem Pole Park: The Kansas Grassroots Art Association, the Foyil Heritage Association, Dr. Carolyn Comfort and Jim Reed and the other members of the Rogers County Historical Society, and the many area businesses and individuals who have supported the restoration with products, services, labor, and cash donations throughout the years.

And finally, to the living memory of Nathan Edward Galloway himself, who once wrote, "All my life I did the best I knew, I built these things by the side of the road to be a friend to you." The words make a fitting epitaph for this one-of-a-kind creator, teacher, and gentleman.

PROLOGUE

It stands almost defiantly beside the two-lane highway, a towering stone sentry stretching high into the Oklahoma sky. For generations, it's watched silently as untold cars zipped by, many on their way to Grand Lake O' The Cherokees, a popular recreational area about half an hour down the road. But it's also seen hundreds of thousands of visitors stop and drive in for a better look. Seldom, if ever, have they gone away disappointed.

Ed Galloway's Totem Pole and the 1¼-acre park that surrounds it make up one of America's great roadside attractions. Although it's not quite along Route 66 -- three and a half miles east of it, to be exact, on Highway 28-A out of Foyil, Oklahoma – Mr. Galloway's Totem Pole Park stands as a shining example of not only the kind of place that propels visitors from across the world down our country's Mother Road, but also as a testament to what a single motivated person can accomplish – even one old enough to have retired from a long career.

As the reader will see, while many others have come along through the years to clean, refurbish, and generally spiff up the Totem Pole, retired woodworking teacher Nathan Edward Galloway created and built the 90-foot-tall structure by himself, one bucket of cement at a time. By his own estimation, it took 100 tons of sand and rock, six tons of steel, 28 tons of cement, and several years of his life to get the Totem Pole the way he wanted it. Then, he set about carving every one of the 200 designs that adorn it.

Mr. Galloway also built the 12-sided museum on the grounds, using concrete, rock, and steel, along with a different kind of wood for each side. In addition, every one of the statues that dot Totem

Pole Park was crafted by his own hands. It took nothing less than death to stop him from creating.

In 1961, he wrote to the Oklahoma State Chamber of Commerce, in response to a letter asking for more information about his work. "This is my hobby and my pasttime," he explained, "since I started the Totem Pole in 1937 and finished it in 1948. The carvings and other pieces have been made through the years and I am still making plans for more as I go along. There is no admission and it is open seven days a week."

Well over a half-century after those words were written, they're still true – even the last sentence. Ed Galloway died the year after composing that letter, and, with its guiding light extinguished, the one-of-a-kind creations he left as a legacy for others to enjoy subsequently endured some tough stretches. As the saying goes, however, whatever doesn't kill you makes you stronger, and Ed Galloway's Totem Pole Park has persevered through periods of vandalism, neglect, and rampant thievery to continue as a unique slice of Americana that draws thousands of visitors each year.

This book is about Ed Galloway and the singular vision that led to his Totem Pole Park, which the July 17, 1964 issue of the *Tulsa World* newspaper dubbed "The Disneyland of the Plains." It's also about the effect that Ed Galloway's creation had, and continues to have, on the folks who've visited it over the decades, as well as those lucky enough to have grown up around it. Here, several people who knew Mr. Galloway contribute to a portrait of the fascinating man behind Totem Pole Park, and Ed Galloway himself weighs in via newspaper accounts and a taped interview from the early 1960s.

Through the years, his creation has been called by various names. There's good evidence that Mr. Galloway himself intended for it to be known as the largest totem pole in the world, which it may well be, Others have called it the largest *man-made* (as opposed to being carved out of an existing rock or tree) totem pole in existence – which it almost certainly is. David Anderson, who manages Ed Galloway's Totem Pole Park with his wife, Patsy, goes with "the world's largest *concrete* totem pole."

"There are a few others around the world that are taller," he explains, "but they're more like thin poles." That makes them different from the Galloway Totem Pole, which, along with being 90 feet high, is 18 feet in diameter and 54 feet around its base.

Whatever you want to call it, Ed Galloway's Totem Pole remains a unique and precious artifact, surrounded and set off by his Totem Pole Park, just as the setting of a ring surrounds and complements a gemstone. The story of how it all began, grew, and almost died, only to live again, is as intriguing and unforgettable as the park itself.

John Wooley
Foyil, Oklahoma
April 2014

CONTENTS

ACKNOWLEDGMENTS

The author and the directors of Ed Galloway's Totem Pole Park want to thank the following people for their help in putting this book together. Their knowledge and willingness to share made this true-life tale of Nathan Edward Galloway, his life, and his lasting creations a far better work than it otherwise would have been.

Leon Anderson, Donald Bryant, Dr. Carolyn Comfort, Ruth Ellen Henry, Bobby Holman, Elwyn Isaacs, Norman Shaw, and Daris and Sue Stimson provided us with clippings, photos, minutes of pertinent meetings, memorabilia, and other material relating to Mr. Galloway and his creations. Some of it, we know, was rare material that hadn't seen the light of day for many years. Mr. Anderson should be singled out for his research into some formerly unknown aspects of Mr. Galloway's military service; he unearthed information that was more than 100 years old, correcting a couple of misconceptions along the way.

In addition to the people mentioned above, we are grateful to Marshall Daugherty, Mary Jane Delozier, Susan Ellerbach, Wilma Fraley, Robert Gideon, Debbie Jackson, Steve Jones, Brenda Horner Lewis, Lee Main, Gerry Payne, Hilary Pitman, Jody Rogers, Suzanne Galloway Rogers, Arden Sanderson, Cilla Wolfe, Laura Wolff, Billie Medlock Wood, and James Vance.

Also helpful were Kenna Carmon, public information manager at the Oklahoma Department of Transportation, and the holdings of the Rogers County Historical Society, the Tulsa City-County Library, and the *Tulsa World*.

Again, our thanks to everyone who helped us in any way, and our sincere apologies if we inadvertently left your name off this list.

CHAPTER ONE

People would come out here and have picnics. This would've been around the 1954-55 time frame, when I was six or seven years old. There were quite a few families around here that came out to sit down and have picnics. They'd cut a watermelon, and just kind of spend a leisurely time underneath the trees. They'd lay out pallets and blankets, quilts on the ground, and some of the older gents would tell stories and the younger kids would sit and listen. Mr. Galloway would walk around and talk to different people. It was quite enjoyable.
- Marshall Daugherty, visiting Ed Galloway's Totem Pole Park during the 2013 Totem Pole BBQ and Music Fest

A great deal of the appeal of Ed Galloway's Totem Pole Park has to do with appreciating tradition, and one of the traditions that's appreciated annually is the use of the park as a picnic spot. Of course, individuals and families can and do use it nearly year-round as a site for alfresco dining, but the first Saturday of every October, hundreds travel there to be a part of the Totem Pole BBQ and Music Fest, overseen by directors David and Patsy Anderson for the Rogers County Historical Society. It's the park's only fundraising event, and those who attend find just about every one of their senses engaged. On that day, the smell of barbecued pork wafts through the park, combining with the imposing sight of the Totem Pole and other one-of-a-kind structures and the sounds of acoustic musicians, jamming together in ad hoc groups throughout the crowd.

In keeping with the spirit of Ed Galloway's Totem Pole Park, the lunches are homemade, with the Andersons and their friends and relatives taking care of everything from smoking the meat to making the cole slaw, baked beans, and cookies that accompany each barbecue sandwich sold. That same group also does the selling.

"You don't want to be our friend or a family member when this comes along," says David Anderson with a laugh.

Patsy picks up the raw materials for those friends and family members to turn into the mass lunch each year. A recent grocery list of hers included 145 lbs. of pork, along with 18 lbs. of cabbage and six lbs. of both carrots and onions, the latter for cole slaw. In addition, she and those helping her cooked up seven gallons of baked beans and 23 dozen cookies. Just about the only things the group members didn't make themselves were the cases of pop and packages of sandwich buns.

The "music" part of the Totem Pole Park BBQ and Music Fest has a similarly homegrown quality, with musicians from all over coming in with their instruments and seeking out like-minded players who know the same tunes – or are at least willing to learn them.

"We put out the word that acoustic pickers are welcome," says Patsy, "and they just show up and do their thing."

So do others from all around the area, drawn by the food and fellowship. Many first visited the Totem Pole when they were kids and are now the "older gents" Marshall Daugherty referred to in the quote that begins this chapter. Like those gents, they enjoy swapping stories about the place and their connections to it.

"I came out here in '48 and '49 a lot," says Norman Shaw, who grew up and now lives in nearby Chelsea. "I was even out here before [the Totem Pole] was done, maybe in '47, when I was a freshman in high school. We'd come out because it was a good thing to do, and he [Mr. Galloway] was a good guy, and he'd tell you stories."

Billie Medlock Wood also remembers a time before the Totem Pole was completed, and especially recalls how Mr. Galloway singlehandedly and laboriously constructed it. She was in a good position to know; during the time the structure was being built, her family had leased a house from the Galloways, just behind where the Totem Pole now stands.

"There used to be a creek that ran down here," she says, pointing to a spot well beyond and downhill from the park, back toward Foyil. "That's where he got the sand and all to make the cement to build that thing. I remember him pushing that wheelbarrow with the sand in it from the creek down there to up here, where he made his cement. And I remember watching him as he finished the Totem Pole. That would've been in 1948."

"We used to come here when I was a little bitty girl, five or six years old," adds Mary Jane Delozier, whose mother was a cousin of Ed Galloway. "I remember coming down here and seeing him pour a bucket of cement. He was making the Totem Pole at the time. This would probably be '40, '41, '42, somewhere in there."

By the time Brenda Horner Lewis came along, the Totem Pole had been standing for some time, and the tradition of visiting the park for picnics had been handed down to her from an earlier generation.

"I've lived around here for 52 years, and I remember first coming out here with my grandma and grandpa when I was six or seven," she says. "We'd come out and have a picnic. It was wonderful out here. Then, when I was 14 and 15, we could walk up to the very top of it. It had stairs inside, all the way up."

While the Totem Pole was the anchor of the park, and the ultimate symbol of Ed Galloway's creativity and indefatigability, he's remembered by longtime visitors for much more – especially the 12-sided fiddle house and the instruments that once hung on the walls within it, all handcrafted by the man himself.

"One of the things Ed would say was that he had, oh, maybe 30 or 40 fiddles started, and he was waiting on wood he'd ordered from all over the country – all over the *world,* really – because of the different colors of the wood," remembered Norman Shaw. "Gosh, he had bunches of 'em that couldn't be completed until a certain color of wood came in. Then he would cut it, machine it, form it, and glue it on."

"There were two [Galloway] brothers, Ed and Charlie," adds Mary Jane Delozier. "Charlie *played* the violins, and Ed *made* them. "Charlie was older, and he could just pick up a violin and play it. Never had a lesson. "With all that different wood, Ed could just make anything. He loved the violins, but then his dream, you know, was to make that Totem Pole."

With that, we leave the enticing scent of barbecue and sound of acoustic music to find out a bit more about the man who not only dreamed of building the world's largest totem pole, but who, singlehandedly and against significant odds, did just that.

As we'll see, those were far from the only long odds Nathan Edward Galloway faced in his life – and with his art.

CHAPTER TWO

Ed Galloway was an unusual man. Then again, anyone who spent eleven years constructing a ninety-foot-tall totem pole would be considered slightly unusual.
– Urbane Chaos, "Totem Pole Park in Foyil, Oklahoma: A Tribute to Native America," posted 22 August 2012 at urbane-chaoshubpages.com

Ed Galloway biographies and fact sheets tend to list his birthplace as "near Springfield, Missouri," although one has him coming into the world in Scotland – not the country, but the Missouri town much closer to Joplin than Springfield – and another in Stone County, 40 miles southwest of Springfield. We do know he had a connection to the latter area; when the county came into being in 1851, it was named after his great-grandfather, W.M. Stone, who also became its first judge.

That's according to an interview recorded circa 1961 by Mr. Galloway's son Paul and transcribed much later by Tim Brown of Austin, Texas, the man who also wrote the text for the audio tour of Totem Pole Park. In the interview, Mr. Galloway notes – among many other things – that his grandfather, Charles Galloway, was serving as a captain in the Union army when he was killed, about 25 miles from Springfield, by bushwhackers, those Confederate guerrilla fighters who were particularly concentrated in the Missouri area during and even after the Civil War.

Charles's youngest son, Nathaniel, was born in 1863, right in the middle of that war. He would go on to marry Cordelia Gideon and move onto what Ed Galloway called in the interview, "a little creek" in Missouri called the Silver Lake Branch.

"He built a log house there, and I was born then," Mr. Galloway said. "I was born in eighteen and eighty, on February the 18th, and we lived there until I was close to six years old."

(Please note that in the quotes from the Galloway interview, English and/or syntax may have been changed slightly from its transcribed form for clarity, without altering the meaning of the words.)

The audio tour of Ed Galloway's Totem Pole Park calls Nathaniel Galloway a "blacksmith and laborer." Like many others living in that time and place, he was also a farmer, at least on the subsistence level, and undoubtedly did other work as well.

Young Nathan Edward Galloway began attending school at the age of six, starting his education at the colorfully named Possum Trot schoolhouse. From there, the family moved to a place owned by his maternal grandfather, Harvey Jim Gideon, near the town of Clever. A couple of years later, Mr. Galloway remembered, they'd moved to a place called the Wolf Den Still House, where his father became involved in distilling whisky. Apparently, that illegal enterprise didn't last long, because the family was soon back on the Gideon place.

"While I was there," Mr. Galloway recalled, "I had to do a crop for my father. He was sick. And I went out and raised my corn, beans, cabbage, and whatever I had to have to support the family – fruits and berries."

He ran into a bit of a windfall when a man named Craig offered him "a little piece of ground" for free, providing young Galloway would clean it up. He did.

> I raised on it a cane patch; it was the most money I'd ever seen. It was on new ground, rich. I hauled it to a fellow named Maples, and he made it into molasses. I had eighty gallons of molasses out of this patch. I brought it back home – my part of it, forty gallons – and I sold some of it to my grandfather, and I took the money and bought the first suit of clothes I'd ever had.

Ed Galloway's Totem Pole Park

Martin Wiesendanger, in a brief biography archived by the Rogers County Historical Society, wrote that the "molasses" Mr. Galloway referred to here was distilled into whisky, indicating that his father wasn't the only family member who flirted with the illegal-spirits business. (One can also infer that Grandfather Gideon had a hand in it as well, unless he was buying for his own consumption.)

By the time the sugar cane opportunity came along, somewhere during his early teens, Ed Galloway had also begun his first tentative steps toward sculpting. It was on the Gideon place, he remembered, that he first began his "little carvings."

"I carved buttons for big coats, made out of mother-of-pearl," he said, "and made wooden buttons that [took] covers of different cloths and things like that. And I made a pretty nice little livelihood for the family with it."

Although it's not clear how much the rest of the family depended on young Galloway for subsistence, his youthful contributions were probably important. Toward the end of his schooling, which was finished after he completed the eighth grade, he began working with his father in the blacksmithing business – hammering out, he recalled, the points of farmers' plowshares just about every evening.

At some point after leaving school, Ed Galloway rebelled, running away from home with a friend. Soon, however, he was back, gathering up "a lot of wood for my father and mother, to do them for the rest of the winter." He then headed to the Springfield area, where he worked on a farm for his uncle. By the time that job was over, his father had gotten into the mining business, and for the next several years Mr. Galloway drove teams for his father and others, hauling lumber, gravel, zinc, and lead. One of his employers, he remembered, was named Bill Willhide, who had "a big team, the best team I'd ever seen pull."

"I took [Willhide's] team and hauled lumber 60 feet long," he said, "and about 16 feet at the base . . . to make these derricks that they used to pull minerals out of the ground with, and to crush [them] and run it 'way off out of the way [to] what they call a gravel pile."

By this time, his mother had died of typhoid fever, and his father had taken the younger children and moved with them back to the Gideon place near Clever. Ed's older brother, Charlie – the one who would later inspire him to try his hand at making fiddles – was by that time performing with a touring show and was seldom home.

Soon, it would be time for Ed Galloway to leave Missouri as well. His reason, however, didn't have anything to do with show business, although it may have had something to do with a woman.

* * * *

Bill Willhide sold out and moved to Barry County, Missouri, on Flat Creek. My [future] father-in-law moved down on Flat Creek, and he had a daughter named Viola, a boy named Louis, a girl named Dori, a girl by the name of Lilly, and a girl named Villie. In Lawrence County one time, I got acquainted with Villie, so I went down there to see her, and we got engaged to be married when I came back from the Army.
– Ed Galloway, from his interview with Paul Galloway,
circa 1961

In the eighteenth year of Nathan Edward Galloway's life, while he was laboring at various jobs in the little piece of America he'd occupied since his birth, the country around him found itself at war. While the conflict with Spain only lasted for about ten weeks, the results of what came to be known as the Spanish-American War were wide-ranging and profound, dropping the final curtain on the Spanish Empire and giving the U.S. authority over Puerto Rico, Guam, and the Philippine Islands, all of which had belonged to Spain.

Revolutionaries in the Philippines, however, who'd begun fighting against Spain a couple of years before the Spanish-American War, viewed the United States as just another country standing in the way of Filipino independence. So, the revolutionary government of the Philippines declared war on America in June 1899, less than a year after the end of the U.S. war with Spain.

The Philippine-American War would last until 1902, taking the lives of more than 4.000 American troops and many more Filipino fighters and civilians. And as that war raged some 8,000 miles away from his home in southwestern Missouri, Mr. Galloway signed up for a stretch in the military, becoming one of the thousands of American men sent to the Philippine Islands to fight.

We can only speculate about why he enlisted. Because there was a war on and young men were needed, perhaps patriotism and a sense of duty to his country had something to do with it. Maybe he was tired of the mining business and the other jobs he'd been doing, or perhaps the work had played out. It's possible that Mr. Hooten and his daughter Villie – Mr. Galloway's new fiancee – had encouraged him.

Whatever the reason, Ed Galloway decided to become a soldier. The day he signed up, as he recalled to his son in their interview, Villie and Mr. Hooten saw him off to the recruiting station.

"I spent part of the day in Aurora [Missouri] with her and her father," he said, "and then I went to Joplin. I had an uncle out there [who had] promised to go into the Army with me, but his sister talked him out of it. So I went over to Joplin and enlisted on the thirtieth day of May 1901 in the United States Army."

Like many other recruits, he was destined for the Philippines. But even before he boarded the ship for those Pacific islands, Mr. Galloway was at least peripherally involved in another historical event. While he was training in Idaho, during September 1901, President William McKinley was assassinated.

"We had a ceremony then," he remembered, "our officers all gathered up, flags raised."

Eventually, Mr. Galloway shipped with Company E of the newly formed 28th Infantry Regiment to the Philippines, the ship stopping off in Honolulu to replace a boiler that had been lost in a storm at sea. It took 41 days for the troops to make it to Manila Bay, where, under then-Captain John J. Pershing, they were put to work constructing a 52-mile stretch of road on the Philippine island of Mindanao, finishing at a large body of water called Lake Lanao.

"While we was building it, a little incident happened with a hunting trip," Mr. Galloway related in his interview. "I and a little boy by the name of Kemp, from St. Jo[seph], Missouri, went out to kill some hogs. He was a butcher. So we went out to kill a wild hog, and we was sitting by this path. I saw something coming, and I said, `I see something comin' down this path, Kemp. I believe I'll shoot at it and see what it is.'

"So I shot, and this thing just kept a-comin', until it got to where we were, and I said, `Don't shoot at it until it passes.' And when it passed, he fired a time or two and that deranged it. It run out into a thicket of vines and couldn't get through. It had a broken leg.

"We went out and shot it then, bled it and cleaned it good and hung it up high enough where the animals wouldn't get to it. We went back and got some boys to come in and get it – it weighed too much for two fellers to carry – and we had it for a feast."

Then, he recalled, along came Captain Pershing, who asked, "Where'd you get the deer?"

Somebody mentioned the circumstances, and, according to Mr. Galloway, "[Pershing] said, `Now listen, boys. There are a whole lot of boys getting killed around here. I don't want to catch you out of this camp anymore, hunting.'"

Mr. Galloway laughed. "He raked me over the coals two or three times about that."

The general was right about the perils faced by the troops on road detail. During the operation, Mr. Galloway lost a friend of his named Keasley, who was, along with several others in his company, overcome by hostile forces on the shore of Lake Lanao. "Keasley was on guard, and these other boys, and the night was damp. Foggy," he said. "Natives came up in boats on that lake and massacred those boys."

Things got even more dangerous when, following completion of the road, Galloway's group was sent to Jolo Island, in a mountainous archipelago in the southern Philippines, where American forces and Filipino revolutionaries were engaged in battle. The U.S. soldiers, Mr. Galloway recalled, "were hemmed in with a big wall around them . . . [they] couldn't get out, and the natives didn't have enough people to break the wall and get in." When the Filipino soldiers tried to scale the walls, he added, the Americans would "shoot 'em off."

"But they kept comin' in such gangs," he added, that the American military feared there would be a massacre. So, under the command of General Leonard Wood – another well-known military leader, who would later become Governor General of the Philippines – Mr. Galloway and his fellow soldiers approached the fighting from the south end of the island, slogging through mangrove swamps to get there. He remembered that volcanic ash from the mountains had turned the water in the rivers and streams around them white, making their depths impossible to gauge.

"General Wood was with us, and the general says, `Here's a good place to cross this stream, boys' – and he stepped off into it plumb up to his arms," remembered Mr. Galloway. "The boys helped him out, and we went on up into the mountains then and got engaged in some skirmishes. A little fellow named Simpson from up in Springfield, Missouri, was stabbed with a knife by a native who stepped out from behind a tree. So we went up on top of this hill to bury him, and we got into another engagement with 'em."

While still on Jolo, Mr. Galloway encountered another historical figure, as he remembered in the interview. "We went down where this camp was, and while we was there, Alice Roosevelt came in with a bunch of officers from different regiments, inspecting our outfit."

Then only a teenager, Alice Roosevelt was the daughter of President Theodore Roosevelt, who'd been McKinley's vice-president before the assassination. Almost from the time her father had assumed the presidency, she had become a very visible symbol of the Roosevelt administration.

"She took a liking to this little pony I'd found," Mr. Galloway said. "I had to go and turn it over to the authorities, and I got to talk a few minutes with Miss Alice Roosevelt."

* * * *

It was there [in the Philippine Islands] that he was introduced to the intricacies of Japanese and Far Eastern art. Many of the alligators and other tropical animals he saw and battled while in the Philippines were later prominent features of his work.
– from "Totem Pole Park," a Rogers County Historical Society fact sheet

After numerous other adventures as a soldier in the Philippines, including a short stint of panning for gold in island streams and a couple of evenings of guarding prisoners and watching natives knock bats out of the sky and eat them, Mr. Galloway returned to the States on a transport ship, landing at the Presidio military base in San Francisco. A private throughout his military career, even while he'd served as Fifth Company mechanic, he was finally promoted to corporal at Presidio, just as his time in the Army was winding down.

Serving out the last few months of his stint in San Francisco, Mr. Galloway was discharged on May 29, 1904, and headed off to much more familiar territory – the government paid for his return to Joplin, where he'd enlisted two years earlier.

Like a lot of newly released soldiers, he had some home folks to visit, not the least of whom was his fiancee, Villie Hooten, then living in Catale, a town in northeastern Oklahoma about 80 miles southwest of Joplin. After a break to visit his father, then running a grocery store in Stockton, Missouri, he returned to Catale to pick up his wife-to-be. The two were married on June 6, at a shop in Carthage, Missouri called the Bolton Baggage Store.

For the next few years, Mr. and Mrs. Galloway spent stretches of time in a number of different southwestern Missouri and northeastern Oklahoma areas. He worked in the mines around Stockton, returned to the Gideon place to help his maternal grandfather and grandmother on the farm, and ran a "contract shop" in Bushyhead, Oklahoma, "building furniture and sharpening plows, shoeing horses, repairing wagons and farm implements." He and Villie were living in that northeastern Oklahoma town around the time of Oklahoma's 1907 statehood – he remembered being on the Bushyhead election board – and likely stayed there through at least 1908.

After Bushyhead, he and Villie moved to the southern Missouri town of Gainesville, and, according to his interview, that's where he "began my searching for timbers to do my carvings."

"It was on the James River that I found my timber," he added. "Then, after I got my timber located, I moved to Springfield, Missouri, worked in a railroad shop for about nine months, and went back to this place [on the river] with my wife and my father-in-law and her uncle, and cut this tree. We moved it in a wagon to Bailey Street near Springfield Avenue, and that's where I began my carving on this piece of timber."

In the extensive interview Mr. Galloway did with his son, this is the first mention he made of his artwork, except for the button-carving he did as a youth. Left unaddressed is the reason for his decision to began sculpting wood in the first place. Hints of what motivated him have to be found in other places – including the book *A Fool's Enterprise: The Life of Charles Page* by Opal Bennefield Clark, first published in 1988 by the Dexter Publishing Company of Sand Springs, Oklahoma. (Oilman and philanthropist Page would have a profound effect on Mr. Galloway's art and life, as we'll see in the next chapter.) Author Clark describes the initial meeting between Galloway and Page in the summer of 1914, after Page had admired the carving of a giant snake coiled around a sycamore log that was being displayed in Getman's Drug Store in Tulsa:

> "How did you ever get into this kind of work?" Mr. Page asked. Mr. Galloway explained in a slow measured drawl. "I spent several months working for the government in Japan and in the Philippine Islands where I became interested in Japanese art. In studying the wood carvings, I decided to try my hand at the art.

(It should be noted that, by Mr. Galloway's own account, he only spent a few days in Japan, with his transport ship stopping in the port of Nagasaki somewhere around Christmas of 1902 on its way back to San Francisco. However, he undoubtedly could've encountered plenty of Japanese carvings during his time in the Philippines.)

The text goes on to explain how Mr. Galloway's art was "discovered," with the Getman's druggist telling the story:

> "Galloway worked in the Springfield Wagon Factory in Springfield, Missouri. Whenever he could get away from his work he went fishing. While waiting for the fish to bite, he would take his pocket knife and carve on any limb or log that happened to be near. Some businessmen from St. Louis who fished in the same stream saw one of

the carvings. They recognized it as a wren. `Who carved that bird?' they asked about town. `An odd young man by the name of Galloway does things like this all the time,' said one of a bunch of fellows standing on the street corner. They told the men where Galloway could be found. One of the men went to talk to Galloway. `Did you carve that wren on a log?' asked the man. Galloway replied, `The wren was in the knot on the log. I just cut the knot away to let him out.'"

Another book, *Sand Springs, Oklahoma: A Community History*, published in 1994 by the Sand Springs Museum, notes that during Mr. Galloway's time at the wagon factory in Springfield, "he would go to the James River and find just the right trees to make what he called `massive pieces' or `statues.' These were large figures made out of tree trunks – in the shape of a hunter, a woman on a throne, and totem poles with figures of animals, fish, and reptiles."

In Opal Bennefield Clark's account, one of the St. Louis businessmen suggested that Mr. Galloway exhibit his work at the Panama Pacific International Exhibition, a world's fair that was to celebrate the upcoming completion of the Panama Canal. Her book *A Fool's Enterprise* has Mr. Galloway explaining it this way:

> "The man offered to secure space for me to display my work at the Panama-Pacific international exhibition to be held in San Francisco in 1915. I was to represent Missouri. He wanted me to produce twenty carvings of large size in the same quality of workmanship as the wren he had seen at the fishing hole, tablets with the busts of the twenty-eight presidents of the United States, a collection of a thousand different colors of wood from within the state of Missouri.
>
> "I selected and cut trees from forests all around the state and had them shipped back to Springfield. I rented a building[,]set up my shop and started working."

Other sources indicate that it was not out-of-town businessmen, but a Missouri state senator from right there in Springfield, Kirk Hawkins, who was so taken by Mr. Galloway's sculpting that he offered to send him to the upcoming world's fair. In that narrative, Senator Hawkins spotted some Galloway work in the window of a Springfield dry-goods shop, where it was being displayed.

"In front of this piece of work, at Red's Dry Goods Store on the square, I met Senator Hawkins," Mr. Galloway recalled in his interview. "He suggested [that] if I'd take it to the San Francisco Fair, they'd pay transportation, [give me a] free concession in the Missouri building, and a year's expense. So I told him I'd go back to the river and make it worth their while by carving some more massive pieces."

Probably, the full story of why he began sculpting in earnest has something to do with both of those stories. In the above-cited interview, he mentions how, "because of one fellow that I met in Springfield, [his] name was Littmann," he decided to rent a studio and put more of his work on exhibit in that space. Littman, of course, could've easily been one of those St. Louis men who encountered Mr. Galloway's work on the banks of a river near Springfield. He may even have told Senator Hawkins about Mr. Galloway's carvings.

However it happened, Mr. Galloway began sculpting in earnest. Before having his creations exhibited at Red's, he'd held onto his day job with the Springfield Wagon Factory, crafting his sculptures by night. He may have continued at the factory after that, although even for a man with Mr. Galloway's work ethic, it would've been tough to hold down a full-time job and create the intricate and massive pieces he did over the next few years in his workshop in the Lands Building, most of which was occupied by the Waters-Pierce Oil Company.

In *A Fool's Enterprise,* Mr. Galloway tells Charles Page that he was to take both completed and nearly finished pieces to San Francisco, working on the latter while he was there, apparently to attract visitors to the Missouri portion of the exhibition. "I had worked on them for four years. Twelve were ready, and the rest nearing completion when a fire broke out in the building."

Among the carvings lost in the blaze was one of a fisherman sitting on a stump with his catch surrounding him, another of a hunter with a stack of game at his feet, and a third one, which he remembered as being "nine feet high [with] a reptile on it about 20 some-odd feet long." At least one photo exists of this strange piece, which features a huge black snake wrapped around the figure of a woman. The model was one of Mr. Galloway's sisters-in-law, Dori Hooten.

"This fire was caused by Waters-Pierce Oil Company, just east of me," he told his son, Paul, in their interview. "While this fire was going on, why, I saw that I couldn't save my big pieces, so I had to push the one that's now in the Sand Springs Home – it's a reptile and fish work with about 30 things on it – through the window, and it rolled down the street. . . .

"I followed it out, and it looked like a beer barrel! It rolled down the street, and you can see the gravel pits in the piece of work today, where the gravel on the street mashed in on it."

The saved piece was the sculpture on display in Getman's Drug Store when Charles Page happened onto it in the summer of 1914. According to Thomas Arthur Repp's 1999 book *Route 66: The Empires of Amusement* (Mock Turtle Press), it had ended up in Tulsa because of Mr. Galloway's determination to get to San Francisco with at least one of his pieces. Wrote Repp:

> In spite of his workshop fire, Galloway decided to attend the Panama Pacific International Exposition. He took his surviving sculpture – a 29-foot reptile wrapped around a sycamore tree – and loaded it onto a westbound train. In Tulsa, Galloway stopped to visit friends and find money.

He housed the sculpture in a drugstore on Archer Street. Sand Springs philanthropist Charles Page passed by the store window and saw the wood carving. So taken was Page with the carving's craftsmanship that he appointed Galloway manual training teacher at the Charles Page Home for Widows and Orphans.

The Panama Pacific International Exhibition went off as scheduled, beginning on February 20, 1915, just about six months after the official opening of the Panama Canal. Since the fair was built partly in the area of the Presidio, Mr. Galloway would've been able to revisit the place where he'd been discharged from the military 11 years earlier.

But, by all accounts, neither he nor his massive snake-centered piece made it to the West Coast. According to *A Fool's Enterprise*, Mr. Galloway had – with some difficulty – loaded it into a wagon the day after meeting Page and sent it to the philanthropist with a note: "To Mr. Page, for his children's home."

Mr. Galloway would follow his sculpture to the Home, where he'd stay for two decades, beginning as one of Charles Page's right-hand men, and staying on to mentor a generation of the youngsters Charles Page called his "kids."

Musicians at the annual BBQ/Music Fest

Annual BBQ/Music Fest volunteers serving BBQ

Jim Reed and Dr. Carolyn Comfort, Past Directors of the Totem Pole Park

Author John Wooley with wife Janis interviewing local Historian Calvin Hardage for this book

Ed showing picture made from different inlaid
woods, a beautiful inlaid chest , and some of
the over 300 fiddles he carved to illustrate
different kinds of wood from around the world.
Many are currently on display in the Gift Shop

Lion in a cage, carved
out of a single log

Early picture of Ed and Villie
taken in Catale, Oklahoma

"The Woman and the Snake":1912-13. Carved for the 1915 San Francisco World's Fair, destroyed in the Springfield fire	Mr. Galloway with the large carving of a 29-foot reptile. The only carving rescued from the Springfield fire

Ed at work building the large Totem Pole -1940's

Totem Pole in 1941

Above: Large Totem Pole and smaller totem with five civilized tribes and plains Indians
Right: Totem Pole as it stands today
Lower: close-up of several of the over 200 Indian images on the large Totem

The 12-sided Fiddle House Ed also used as a workshop

The park became deserted and rundown after Ed's death in1962

Restoration in 1990s by
Kansas Grass Roots
Association

Adding the finishing touches
to the 90-foot Totem Pole

Nine foot tall Indian
Chiefs, facing each
cardinal direction, top
the large Totem Pole

Original gate posts of
fence surrounding the
Park

CHAPTER THREE

Mr. Page was a brilliant man, so he knew not only good work, but he knew good people*. He wanted to surround himself and his kids – which is what he called them, not orphans, but his kids – with the best people, who would not only teach them a trade, but teach them a way of life. And that's what Mr. Galloway did.*
– Ruth Ellen Henry, former director of the Sand Springs Museum, in an interview for this book

In 1905, Wisconsin native Charles Page hit pay dirt with a well in Indian Territory that began pumping out 2,000 barrels of oil a day. Then living in the territorial boom town of Tulsa with his wife and child, he became a millionaire fairly quickly and, in 1908, the year after Indian Territory was incorporated into the new state of Oklahoma, Page used a portion of his new wealth to buy 160 acres west of the city.

Because of his father's declining health and early death, Page had quit school at the age of 10 and gone to work to support his mother and his four siblings. According to his online Wikipedia biography, Page "knew first-hand how fatherless children often had to forgo a school education to help support themselves or their families by working full-time in menial jobs . . . . He envisioned creating a planned community where widows and orphans could live and become more productive members of society."

Starting with only a few orphans who had to live in tents, Charles Page soon had several dozen of them housed in a frame building, as he laid the groundwork for what would become his well-known charity, the Sand Springs Home. In 1911, he built a railway – later a trolley line – connecting the area to Tulsa.

"Page also decided to form the City of Sand Springs to the west of the home," wrote Carl N. Gregory in the online *Oklahoma Historical Society's Encyclopedia of Oklahoma History and Culture*. "He offered free land to anyone who wanted to relocate. He established the aforementioned transportation system connecting Tulsa and Sand

Springs and offered companies a twenty-thousand-dollar relocation bonus." (In her 1999 book *Sand Springs, Oklahoma*, historian Jayme Landis writes that the name of the town was chosen because it was "in an area known for its clear water from several `sandy springs.'")

Upon its incorporation in 1912, Sand Springs had a population of around 400, including the staff and children at the Sand Springs Home.

Two years later, Nathan Edward Galloway and Charles Page encountered one another for the first time. The meeting seems to have happened pretty much the way Opal Bennefield Clark — one of Page's many "kids" — described it in *A Fool's Enterprise,* the book referred to in our last chapter. In his interview with son Paul, Mr. Galloway remembered meeting the Sand Springs founder in the Tulsa drugstore that was temporarily housing his snake sculpture, and subsequently being asked by Page to visit his office. There, the philanthropist told Mr. Galloway about his orphans' home and, apparently, offered him a job right on the spot.

> I told him what I'd like to do with the boys, because I thought I could handle them, and he told me how many he had. There were about 30.
>
> He said, `Well, it's awful hot now to build a house, and we don't have any out there that we can rent you or settle you [in]." So I went back to Catale, where my wife was. . . and I worked for a feller named Faye Bearden, building some barn doors. Then I drove a team and a mowing machine, mowing prairie hay. I returned back to Sand Springs on the first of September [1914] and began my building there with two carpenters. I helped to build my own building.
>
> We finished this building up, and I got my wife and brought her down there. Then, Mr. Page gave [me] what is called the old Empel Building . . . for a workshop.

Mr. Galloway wasted no time putting his charges to work. As the Home's new manual-training instructor, he began helping them build, he recalled, "wagons, singletrees, tongues, all kinds of farming implements." A couple of years later, in 1916, he helped construct the Home's new two-story manual training shop, made out of native sandstone. When it was finished, Charles Page and the Home's administrators bought loads of new machinery for the shop. From that location, Mr. Galloway said, "We made every conceivable thing you could think of out of wood. We made all kinds of boxes for fruits, all kinds of dollies for the cotton mill, all kinds of furniture for the Home. . . . We made lots of little articles that were sold just at cost to people in Tulsa, and shipped to foreign countries. . . . "

"It was one of the largest and best equipped buildings for shop work in the southwest," wrote Clark, adding:

> The boys undertook the repair work about the Home. They made some of the garden tools, rakes, and other devices such as wheelbarrows and carts. Later they mended the furniture. Many became so good at it that thereafter they built most of the furniture for the Home. At Christmas time each year they made cedar chests, inlaid sewing boxes and various gifts for the girls of the Home to receive from Santa. They also made many fine elaborately carved articles.

Nineteen-fourteen was also the year that Charles Page established a "widows' colony," for mothers without husbands, at the Home. As *Sand Springs, Oklahoma: A Community History* tells us, "[A] few small cottages consisting of two rooms each (known as box car houses) were built by boys from the Home under Mr. Galloway's supervision. Furniture was supplied, if necessary. The mothers were encouraged to seek employment, and a small one-room cottage was made to house a day nursery."

Less functional, but probably more fun, were the "many odd things" (Mr. Galloway's term) that he and the boys made for Charles Page's Sand Springs Park, an 80-acre amusement area featuring such attractions as a Ferris wheel, roller coaster, merry-go-round, and herds of deer, antelope, and buffalo. Among other things, Mr. Galloway did the paintings for the sides of the merry-go-round and served as roller-coaster inspector. Although he used "we" when talking about who worked on the pair of 10-ton sandstone lions made for the park, they were undoubtedly crafted largely by Mr. Galloway, with a little help from his students. (After guarding the entrance of the Sand Springs Park for years, the statues were moved to the Sand Springs Home's entrance, where they still stand today.)

In addition to being their teacher, Mr. Galloway served as a father figure for the orphans and fatherless children at the Home. As noted in *Sand Springs Oklahoma: A Community History*, "He took them camping, taught them how to fish, and made sure that they were well trained and had a good time growing up. Those who remember him call him stern but fair – a man who lived by the Golden Rule."

Several former Charles Page Home residents supplied reminiscences for that book, including Asa Davis, whom Ruth Ellen Henry described as "one of the first boys Charles Page brought to Sand Springs." Said Davis:

> We all loved Mr. Galloway. Sometimes he would take us on camping trips. I remember once he took us up above the Shell Creek Dam [constructed in 1920 to supply water to Sand Springs], and he taught us how to drill our own wells for water - Of course, we didn't have to go but four or five or maybe six feet. Another time, he was going to take the boys a little younger than I was to the park. Ray Ritchie, the evangelist, was preaching in Tulsa, and they took the boys over to hear him. For some reason, I wasn't with them. It was pouring down rain, and all the boys prayed that the Lord Jesus would give them clear weather

so we could go to the park with Mr. Galloway. And you know, we did have clear weather, but as soon as we got home from the park, it started pouring down rain again. I didn't know what to think about that. I was afraid it would make the Lord mad.

And Sam McGakey, who arrived at the Sand Springs Home as an orphan in 1918, offered these observations:

We stayed [at the Home] until we made enough money to move out and live somewhere else. The Home always gave us a job to make a living, and it was our privilege to leave there when we were ready. The first job I can remember I had at the Home was working in the manual training shop. The kids could work in there when they were about eight years old doing whatever odd jobs Mr. Galloway could find for us. We would work there before school and after school and half a day on Saturday. We got to play a little bit and then we'd work a while. That's the way Mr. Galloway regulated it. He was one of the best guys I ever met in my life. He was so nice to us kids and he showed us everything to help us. . . .

In the winter Mr. Galloway would take us down to the river bottom. . . and we would cut cedar trees to get logs. We sawed our own lumber. Then he cured it and dried it. The Home still has the furniture we made out there: the chairs and tables in the dining room. There was also a whole living room outfit we made out of solid walnut. One table we made had 3200 pieces of wood in it!

. . . . [E]very Christmas the big girls would get a cedar hope chest that the boys had made for them. They were at least four feet long and 18 foot square. The townspeople would sometimes come out and buy different kinds of stuff that we made, especially nut bowls and salad bowls and little cedar chests. We also built all the hamburger stands at the Park.

> In the summer, Mr. Galloway would take us
> camping on Grand River, the Verdigris River, and
> a place called Briar Creek. We'd camp in tents and
> fish, swim, and just run around. . . .

"Anyone who ever worked with him in his manual woodshop would say that everything he taught them had more than just a woodworking lesson to it," noted Ruth Ellen Henry. "For instance, he had them all make a perfect sphere. It had to be perfect, so it could roll. And as they were doing that, he taught them math, he taught them about the world, he taught them all kinds of lessons."

And in Charles Page's office on the Sand Springs Home grounds, the Galloway sculpture that had inadvertently led to his employment as manual-training instructor also gave Page's kids something a little extra – if they knew where to look.

"It wasn't just a large serpent," said Henry. "It had a butterfly, and a raccoon sticking its head out, and within it there were three little drawers. Sometimes Mr. Page would have pennies in one of the drawers, sometimes he would have peppermints – there was always something for the kids to find. And they always loved to look in those little drawers."

(It's not known whether the drawers always existed in the piece, or if they were added at Page's request, but evidence indicates they're indeed a part of the same sculpture that Galloway rolled down the street and away from the fire that destroyed his Springfield workshop.)

* * * *

During his years at the Sand Springs Home, Galloway bought land in the hills to the northeast of Tulsa that Oklahomans call the Green Country. On weekends and vacations, he and boys from the orphanage camped out and built a stone house, situated between the towns of Foyil and Chelsea. . . .
– from "Ed Galloway's Totem Pole: A Case Study in

Restoration" by Barbara Brackman, in _Backyard Visionaries: Grassroots Art in the Midwest,_ edited by Barbara Brackman and Cathy Dwigans (University Press of Kansas, 1999)

Although Charles Page died of influenza on December 27, 1926, the Sand Springs Home continued. Mr. Galloway continued right along with it, working another decade or so before finally retiring. By that time, by his own account, he'd "put in six years building on the piece of property" he'd bought in an area he knew well – the 20 acres he had were very close to both Bushyhead and Catale, two of the rural Oklahoma towns where he and Villie had lived before moving to Sand Springs.

There were three in the Galloway family now, as they had adopted a son, Paul, back in 1918. Along with boys from the Sand Springs home, he helped gather rocks for the ongoing building of Mr. Galloway's house and did other work around the 20-acre property, on weekends and summers away from the Sand Springs Home. By Mr. Galloway's own account, he "put in six years building" the rock house.

Apparently, he waited until it was finished before giving notice at the Home, although, according to _Route 66: The Empires of Amusement,_ he "attempted retirement" in 1934, only to be called back. The author notes that "in 1937, he finally wiggled free," moving from Sand Springs to his northeastern Oklahoma property with Villie and Paul.

Bobby Holman, whose parents and brother ran a grocery store next to Totem Pole Park for many years, said in an interview for this book that, after leaving Sand Springs, "Mr. and Mrs. Galloway moved to Catale first, and lived in a railroad-tie house up there." He also indicated that Mr. Galloway may have been working on his most famous creation – not just his home – before he and his family actually moved onto the grounds of what is now Totem Pole Park.

Whether he did or not, it took him, by Mr. Galloway's own admission, some 11 years to finish his Totem Pole, doing most of the work by himself. (Said Bobby Holman with a smile, "There wasn't anybody who could do it like *he* wanted to do it, so he didn't want any help.") That kind of dedication, and the one-of-a-kind structure it produced, may seem incredible to many. Maybe, however, it didn't seem quite as unusual to those orphaned kids who'd known him as their manual-training teacher.

"Mr. Galloway had always made totem poles," said Joy Galloway, Paul's widow, in *Route 66: The Empires of Amusement*. "People have forgotten that. At the Sand Springs Home – when a tree died in the yard around the woodshop – he would take out his tools and carve the tree into a totem pole. He would make something beautiful out of it, and leave the dead tree where it stood."

CHAPTER FOUR

"I just wanted to build a totem pole," the wizened Galloway said. **"And I did."**
— George Kane, **"Talent for Wood Carving Produces Vast Collection,"** *Tulsa World*   (Feb. 27, 1962)

What was Nathan Edward Galloway's reason for tackling a project so immense that it would take him over a decade of hard work to complete? Certainly, no one asked him to do it, and, as far as can be ascertained, he had no arts patron supplying him with words of encouragement, much less cash. In fact, his financial circumstances dictated that he scrounge up a lot of the materials he needed to construct his totem pole. The audio tour for Totem Pole Park, written by Tim Brown, calls Mr. Galloway "a notoriously thrifty man, using found and recycled materials throughout the park."

That assessment is seconded by longtime Galloway neighbor and friend Bobby Holman.

"He'd pick up rocks on the way out from Foyil in his old car," recalled Holman, "bring 'em in and put 'em up. That's when he still lived in Sand Springs. And all of his equipment, his carving tools, he'd make out of old files and stuff. He never bought *nothing*."

Other sources, including material submitted by the Rogers County Historical Society to the National Register of Historic Places, noted that Galloway — who at some point became car-less after his move to rural Rogers County — would often hitchhike from his home to the surrounding towns of Claremore, Adair, and Chelsea, collecting pieces of scrap wood and glass from their lumberyards. And a *Tulsa Tribune* story from March 19, 1980, offers this quote from Galloway's son, Paul: "I would get scrap guy wire from the Sand Springs Railway, where I was working at the time. They didn't have any use for it, and were just going to throw it away. We used it as steel reinforcement for the concrete."

Although lifelong area resident Laura Wolff was born only a few years before Mr. Galloway completed the pole, she later saw first-hand evidence of his scavenging skills.

"I remember going out there [to Totem Pole Park] one time, and Daddy telling me, `Look up in there. You'll see some rods coming out at the top.'" she said in an interview for this book. "There was a beautiful sky, and I saw those rods coming out, and he told me that Mr. Galloway had gotten those from him. I think they were to reinforce the top of the totem pole."

"Mother said she could remember him coming out there and picking up this wrought iron," she added. "I don't know how he knew about it, and I don't know if he paid anything. All I know is that Daddy was the person that let him have it."

According to various sources, Mr. and Mrs. Galloway were living on his war pension of $90 a month during much of the time he was working on the Totem Pole, which goes a long way toward explaining his frugal approach to acquiring the materials needed for his work. However, that figure probably isn't exact. And although many references to Mr. Galloway note that his pension was awarded to him for his service in the Spanish-American War, that's not exactly correct, either; as we've seen, he actually served in the Philippine-American War.

Those who've gotten confused on this topic can be forgiven. According to the Spanish-America War Centennial Website (www.spanamwar.com), while the U.S. Government had established funding for Spanish-American War pensions, "A new Philippine American War pension fund was never created. So, men who were involved in fighting as late as 1906 in the Phillippine American War – eight years after the Spanish American War ended – collected Spanish American War pensions!"

At first, those pensions were only given to wounded veterans and the families of war casualties. However, the Sherwood Act of 1912 awarded pensions to all veterans, to begin automatically at age 62. Under that stipulation, Mr. Galloway would've begun receiving $101.59 each month, beginning in 1942. Two years earlier, the U.S. government had begun implementing the new Social Security program, and he would've been in line for those payments as well, starting in 1945 when he turned 65 years old. It's possible that Villie was also Social Security-eligible. So while he was hardly growing wealthy off the government's largesse, Mr. Galloway may have had a little more of a financial cushion than is generally reported, at least after he turned 62. (It's possible that he and Mrs. Galloway lived on savings between 1937, when they moved from Sand Springs, and 1942, when he became pension-eligible, as there's no record of his receiving retirement benefits from the Sand Springs Home.)

Then again, maybe money really *was* tight for the Galloways. In the 1962 *Tulsa World* story that produced the epigraph at the beginning of this chapter, George Kane wrote that Mr. Galloway "even once had to do without a pair of shoes to buy wood and cement for the giant totem pole, but he says it was a pleasure doing without to build something he wanted." (This story may have originated in a 1949 column by Cal Tinney, a writer and humorist in the Will Rogers style, who noted in a *Tulsa Tribune* piece that when Mr. Galloway "needed more money for his art, he just went without shoes.")

Other veterans and retirees may have used their monthly checks from Uncle Sam to help ease them into a more secure and sedate old age, but not Ed Galloway. He took his government money, bought the material that he couldn't scavenge or recycle — like bags of cement — and kept right on going at least as hard as he'd gone before his retirement from the Sand Springs Home. For an incredible 11-year stretch, according to *Route 66: The Empires of Amusement*, "Galloway worked . . . as much as 16 hours a day. Evenings, he returned to his dining room and whittled wooden fiddles – scraping them with broken glass as he sat beside his stove."

He began constructing his Totem Pole in 1937, after he and Villie had moved into the rock house he'd constructed over six years of weekends and vacations away from Sand Springs. As Tim Brown's audio tour puts it:

> Starting from the base of the huge turtle that the Plains Indians thought of as the earth itself, Mr. Galloway built this massive structure up level by level, starting with the base and working his way upwards with six other smaller rooms at a rate of approximately ten feet a year . . . .
>
> . . [A] series of ladders on the inside leading from each small room would help him to scurry up to the top of the pole. Imagine Ed Galloway, with his customary wool hat, khaki slacks and dirty work shirt scurrying up and down the inside of the hollow concrete tube, cranking up buckets with the help of a windlass. Neighbors said it was a sight to be seen.

One who saw the sight from the inside was Suzanne Galloway Rogers, Mr. Galloway's granddaughter. Born in 1938, when Mr. Galloway had just begun working on the Totem Pole in earnest, she spent many youthful summers at her grandparents' home, traveling there from Nome, Alaska, where her father, Paul, was employed.

"My granddad would put me on his back and take me inside the Totem Pole," she recalled in an interview for this book. "We'd go up the ladders, all the way to the top, inside. I was eight or nine years old, and I loved it. I was probably too young to be scared."

Mr. Galloway sank holes at intervals into the pole, using them to secure his scaffolds as he laboriously worked his way upward. And, as was the case with every other aspect of the work-in-progress, he even built the scaffolding his way.

35

"[Chelsea businesswoman] Marie Jay and her husband, Fred, were good friends with Mr. Galloway, and I remember her telling me that the scaffolding platform he used was very narrow," recalled area resident Wilma Fraley in an interview for this book. "When they asked him why, he said it was because he knew just how much room he had for his feet, and he thought that if he made it wider, he might back up, thinking he had plenty of room, and make a misstep. But since it was continually in his mind that he only had that much space, that was that."

"He built it so it was freestanding, and he built it from the inside out, as I recall," added Lee Main, who visited the site with his father several times in the late '40s, before the Pole was completed. "As he would go up, he would go up with his scaffolding on the *inside*. And then, I guess the painting of the icons, or whatever you'd call them, was done from the outside, with scaffolding and ladders and so forth."

A photo published in a 1944 issue of the *Kansas City Star* newspaper gives credence to Main's observation. It's a shot of the unfinished Totem Pole, with 40 feet or so completed and painted and a scaffolding system clearly protruding out of the top from the inside. An accompanying paragraph notes that the Pole encloses Mr. Galloway's "300-gallon water tank. . . [which] supplies the house and is used for sprinkling the lawn."

Daris Stimson, a longtime Foyil real-estate agent, grew up in the area. In an interview for this book, he recalled that his school bus would occasionally take a route that passed Mr. Galloway's work-in-progress.

"About 1940, when I was six or seven," he said, "was just about when he had the turtle [base] done. It seemed like he would go up maybe eight or 10 feet a year. I was grown before he ever got it topped out."

* * * *

Its construction was carefully planned, starting with blueprints. Galloway says he has used 28 tons of cement, which was mixed with three parts water and 50 percent rock. Six tons of steel went into the towering tourist attraction.
— unbylined story from the *Claremore Daily Progress*, June 15, 1955

The Totem Pole may have been "carefully planned," but Mr. Galloway also made part of it up as he went along. At some point, for instance, he got rid of the water tank inside the Pole. If the *Kansas City Star* piece is accurate, he also decided to make it taller than he'd planned by a good third, going up to 90 feet rather than, as the paper reported, the 60 feet he'd originally planned. (Another source, written by Edward Curtis for the April 8, 1941 *Tulsa World*, says, "When completed, the weirdly embellished sides of the pole will tower 50 to 70 feet . . . . Inside will be six rooms, one above the other, all 18 feet in diameter." The Curtis piece does not mention a water tank.)

Mr. Galloway built the Pole by creating a skeleton out of the scrap metal and native rock he'd accumulated, then covering it with the concrete that he'd mixed himself, one bucket at a time, using sand he'd wheelbarrowed up from the nearby creek.

"He had a little old cement mixer, and I think it was powered, at least at first, by a gasoline engine," remembered Main. "He would mix what mud he was going to use that day, and go up the structure with it."

Wrote the *World*'s Curtis, "With a case knife he has sculpted into its wet concrete sides the likenesses of chiefs of the Five Civilized Indian Tribes. In addition, he has added the heroic, grotesque figures which all fashionable totem poles wear . . .

"He already has used 230 sacks of cement and tons of rock in the structure, which will probably be completed in about two years."

In fact, Mr. Galloway worked for about seven more years after the publication of that story, ending with four nine-foot effigies of famous American Indians at the top, each facing a different direction. *Claremore Daily Progress* writer Joe Zodrow described them in his "Smoke Signals" column for November 6, 1960:

> Looking into the rising sun is the peace maker, Chief Joseph, a Nez Pierce; ominously watching the setting sun is the stalwart Apache warrior, Geronimo; gazing severely, yet serenely, to the northward is the champion of the historic Battle of the Little Big Horn, Sitting Bull, Chief of the Sioux; the grave, intelligent man with the winning personality, Chief of the Comanches, Quanah [Parker], the Eagle, scans the horizon into the Lone Star state and all the southland.

According to the date carved in concrete above the door to the Totem Pole's interior, Mr. Galloway finished the job in 1948. The exact day is lost to history – in fact, there may not *be* an exact completion date, since he continued to do work on the Pole and the grounds for years afterwards. He apparently did nothing to celebrate the day his eleven years of labor was completed, no ceremony or party or other acknowledgement.

"Oh, heavens no," said Billie Medlock Wood, who lived for a time as a girl with her parents on the Galloway property. "You didn't do things like that in those days. He finished it, and that was it, and then he started on something else."

But while he continued to build many other things, which we'll look at shortly, it's the Pole that remains the centerpiece of the park to this day, a beautifully improbable attraction, towering over a two-lane Oklahoma highway, that continues to draw visitors from all over the world.

Which brings us back to the question we began with: Why did he do it? What could make a man put well over a decade of hard and mostly singlehanded daily work into creating a 90-foot-tall monument to Native American culture and history? After all, it doesn't seem to have been his *own* history.

"I get asked a lot about that," said Totem Pole Park co-director David Anderson. "And what I always tell people is that we have no evidence of any American Indian ancestry for Mr. Galloway."

"I have always heard that he was full German," added Suzanne Holman Rogers.

In an interview for this book, Totem Pole museum and gift shop employee Cilla Wolfe remembered seeing a snapshot brought to the museum from Kansas City by one of Mr. Galloway's cousins.

"I turned it over, and it said, `1955, my cousin Ed Galloway, one-quarter Cherokee," she remembered. "It makes sense. He *looks* Cherokee. But no one has ever proven it."

Whether or not he had even a drop of American Indian blood running through his veins, preserving the unique heritage and history of the area where he settled was likely one of his major motivations. Lee Main, who spent hours as a teenager listening to his father and Mr. Galloway visit in the shadow of the unfinished Totem Pole, advanced that notion in his interview for this book.

"Looking back, I would say he did it just to say, `I built this so it would be a lasting monument to the Indian heritage and culture in this area. And I did it by myself, with my own two hands.'"

Mr. Galloway himself was not voluble about his reasons for building the Pole and the rest of his creations – at least, not for the record. In his late-in-life interview with his son, he said, "I decided after six years there with the [Sand Springs] Home [while building his house outside of Foyil] that I would come out here and get independent with something, and so I come out and built the Totem Pole."

Many have since speculated on the "why" of the Totem Pole. Writing on the online HubPages site, for instance, Urbane Chaos (at http://urbane-chaoshubpages.com) said, "This massive monument, although generally credited as a monument to American Indian History, was nothing more than a way for Ed to pass the time." Her source may be the previously mentioned 1941 *Tulsa World* story by Edward Curtis, who wrote, "The idea for the unique pole came to him as he cast about for means of spending his idle time," buttressing that theory with a quote from Mr. Galloway: "I guess I could tear in and complete it in three or four months, but I'd rather just work on it when I feel like doing something."

The material submitted to the National Register of Historic Places noted that Mr. Galloway wanted "to let people know there was someone here before us," and that could've been another part of his motivation – although if it was, it wasn't because he took himself and his work too seriously. As he told the *World*'s Curtis, "It's kind of funny when you get to thinking about it. People will find this thing here long after we're dead and speculate on the 'prehistoric Indians' who built such a crazy-looking thing."'

Mr. Galloway's son, Paul, told *Tulsa Tribune* writer Paul C. Day – for a story published March 19, 1980 – that his father "always wanted people to see his work so they could enjoy life more. He said the way to open doors for people was to make something for them." Indeed, his unique contributions to folk art may have been made simply because he got joy out of people seeing and commenting on what he'd done, and because he honestly thought his creations enriched their lives, just as the things he'd made added to the lives of the adults and children connected with the Sand Springs Home. Certainly there was no financial motive, since he never charged admission to Totem Pole Park. As he told George Kane for the previously cited 1962 *Tulsa World* story,

"I don't charge a nickel for people to see this stuff. I like for them to stop and talk and enjoy seeing it. That's worth more than money."

In that spirit, this section closes with an oft-cited couplet from Mr. Galloway, which he allegedly composed on his death bed. "All my life I did the best I knew," he wrote. "I built these things by the side of the road to be a friend to you."

* * * *

The Totem Pole, which is made from twenty-eight tons of cement, six tons of steel, one-hundred tons of sand and rock, is 90 feet high, 18 feet in diameter, 54 feet around the base on which it stands. It has two hundred different carved pictures on it, with four nine foot Indians near the top . . . .
The Museum . . . [a] concrete, rock and steel enforced building, with twelve sides, houses three hundred violins, each made from a different kind of wood. I also have ninety inlaid wood pictures, inlaid tables and a cedar chest in my collection. . . .
– N.E. Galloway, from his reply (dated October 7, 1961) to a letter from the Oklahoma State Chamber of Commerce & Development Council

As mentioned earlier in this chapter, Mr. Galloway didn't stop creating when his workday on the Totem Pole came to an end. Evenings, as well as days when the weather was too dicey to work outside, would find him inside his rock house, carving fiddles and creating other *objets d'art*, including inlaid wood portraits of American presidents. The fiddles, according to Paul Galloway's widow, Joy, grew out of Mr. Galloway's longtime hobby of collecting different kinds of wood.

"The fiddles were really a wood collection," she told *Route 66: The Empires of Amusement* writer Thomas Arthur Repp. "The goal was to carve one fiddle from every kind of wood in the world."

To that end, Mr. Galloway would often advertise his craving for exotic wood in the Sand Springs *Home* newsletter, and his former charges, now grown men living all over the world, would gift their old manual-training instructor presents of chunks of timber from exotic locales.

"I spent 40 years collecting wood," Mr. Galloway told the *Tulsa World*'s Kane. "I spent 23 years carving most of this stuff."

And at some point, Villie told him he needed someplace else to put it.

"He had stuff in the house first, and he'd bring people in all the time to look it over," explained Bobby Holman. "I don't think she liked that too well."

"She told him, `I'm tired of people in my house,'" recalled Joy Galloway for *Route 66: the Empires of Amusement*. "And so he built the Fiddle House."

Added the book's author, Thomas Arthur Repp:

> Galloway constructed his eleven-sided Fiddle House on the east side of Totem Pole Park. He first called his show-place the Grape House for the fruit clusters (and occasional tree frog) carved into its support beams. Murals decorated walls; wood-relief pictures looked out at the world through pieces of white balsam, dark cherry and black teak. Along the back and one sidewall, Galloway hung his fiddles.

(The alert reader will note that Repp calls the Fiddle House an eleven-sided building, while Mr. Galloway, in his letter excerpted above, gives it twelve sides. It all depends on whether you count the outer wall of the building bisected by its door as one side or two.)

In the late '40s, with the Totem Pole completed and the Fiddle House well on its way, those who wanted to visit the area didn't have the smooth two-lane that now characterizes Oklahoma 28-A. "It wasn't even graveled then, let alone paved," recalled Billie Medlock Wood. "It was just mud – a dirt road."

Then, in 1949, Mr. Galloway offered his young neighbor, Joe Holman – who'd recently graduated from high school – an acre of property just east of the Fiddle House.

"Mr. Galloway wanted him to build a little pop stand out there," remembered Bobby Holman, Joe's brother. "Joe tried to pay him for it, but Mr. Galloway wouldn't take anything. He just wanted something out there. So they put a little stand, about 8 by12 [feet], out in front of the Totem Pole. It cost fifty dollars to build."

At the time, according to Wood, workers had begun putting gravel on the road that ran by the Totem Pole, and Joe Holman – who had a birth defect that restricted his mobility – sold soft drinks and other food items to those laborers. Over time, the stand metamorphosed into Little Joe's Grocery.

"He just kept putting stuff in it [the stand], and putting stuff in it, and it got too much," explained Bobby Holman. "So Dad built a store, 16 by 24, up here. Willie Bob Wooten had a team of horses, and he took one of those Fresnos [horse-drawn scrapers used for digging ditches] and cleaned out a place to put it, and Joe kept adding to it.

"Mr. Galloway would make fourteen trips up there a day," Holman added with a laugh. "He'd come up there and sit on that old counter, throw his leg down, and it didn't make any difference if there were customers or not. He'd sit there and visit, and then he'd say, `Well, I've got to go home.'

"He lived on milk, cereal, and quinine – that's what he took for medicine. If he had an ache or pain or felt bad, he'd take a quinine pill. And he'd come up there to the store and get him some milk and Post Toasties."

* * * *

What he made was always first-cabin type stuff. He was very pleasant, and he always had time to stop and talk to you. Maybe that's why it took him so long to build the Totem Pole.
– Norman Shaw, who visited Mr. Galloway frequently in the late '40s and early '50s

The 1950s would be a good decade for Nathan Edward Galloway and his Totem Pole Park – the only full decade both he and his well-known creation would be together. Following the completion of the Fiddle House, he set about making other structures for the park, most of them with American Indian themes. As he told his son, Paul, "I built a tree with a number of things on it, built an arrowhead with the Five Civilized Tribes on it, and [put] the western Indians on the opposite side from the Totem Pole."

During his work of the Pole, he had constructed a picnic table for visitors, which became used more and more as the '50s wore on. There was also a birdbath and birdhouse, built later in the 1950s, the latter crafted to attract mosquito-eating purple martins.

And then there was what the Park's audio tour calls the "Dr. Seuss-like tree structure," which Mr. Galloway referred to in the interview. It was probably the last major thing Mr. Galloway built before his death. Allegedly, he tackled the project after Villie teased him with a rephrasing of the last couplet in Joyce Kilmer's famous poem, "Trees," saying, "Totem poles are made by fools like thee/But only God can make a tree."

"Out of this challenge," wrote Tim Brown for the audio tour, "Galloway built a monument to the nature that surrounded him and also a home for the plethora of birds that inhabited the blackjack, oak, and mimosa trees that covered the property" – a concrete tree about five feet in diameter, decorated like the Totem Pole with images of animals and American Indians.

In the late '40s and very early '50s, recalled Norman Shaw, Mr. Galloway and the park "were more or less taken for granted, I think. There weren't crowds. We'd come out, and he'd be laying a rock or two, or working on his fiddles in the fiddle room. But it wasn't really noted then."

However, by the time Mr. Galloway had completed that final structure in what would become known as Totem Pole Park, word had gradually gotten out and more visitors were arriving – not only from the surrounding towns, but from all over. The locals had learned about the Totem Pole via word of mouth; many of the others had first encountered it in a newspaper or magazine piece. (In his 1961 letter to the Oklahoma State Chamber of Commerce, Mr. Galloway noted that he had "eighty clippings from newspapers, all over the U.S.A." dealing with the Pole, and the major national magazine *Life* also did a spread on his work.)

Still, even as the crowds increased, Mr. Galloway adamantly refused to charge any admission to what he referred to as his Totem Pole and Museum.

"He had a jar up there [in the Fiddle House] for people to put money in, if they wanted to," remembered Bobby Holman. "Once or twice, I think, some kids stole money out of it. But he was pretty lucky." (The author remembers seeing that glass jar on a table inside the Fiddle House in the late 1950s or early 1960s, with a hand-lettered label noting that donations helped pay for the park's electricity.)

Mr. Galloway would also occasionally create, or reconstruct, things for other people, including cedar chests and fiddles. And even then, he took little money in exchange for his craftsmanship. In an undated letter from the Rogers County Historical Society's files, Virgil L

Hoss of Bakersfield, California remembered a piece of work Mr. Galloway did for him.

> I first met Ed when I was in high school in Adair [a town approximately nine miles from Totem Pole Park]. I bought a violin in Pryor [another nearby town] for $2.00. The neck was broken off. I took it over to Ed (I called him Mr. Galloway then), and he fashioned a new neck, fingerboard and tailpiece for it. He also installed patent tuning pegs on it. He carved an Indian face silhouette, side view, in full headdress where the tuning pegs are located. The total cost, including strings and bridge, came to $5.10!

As Mr. Galloway had told the *Tulsa World*'s George Kane – and as Virgil Hoss's story illustrates – having people "stop and talk and enjoy seeing" his work was worth far more than cash. And by early 1962, when the Kane story ran, hundreds of thousands of folks had done just that.

Wrote the *World* reporter:

> Galloway keeps registers which visitors sign. He has a number beside each name in the dozens of registration books, and at last count, he said, he had "almost 400,000 signatures." The towns listed beside each name cover an area from San Francisco to New York, and Canada to Mexico. On weekends, people who brave the wilderness surrounding his land visit at the rate of 200 to 300 a day.

By the time that article came out – on February 27. 1962 – Villie had been gone for nearly two years, dying at the age of 79 following an illness of several weeks' duration. She passed away on May 6, 1960, a month before their 56th wedding anniversary. And while 82-year-old Mr. Galloway sounds upbeat and positive in the *World* story, he would not survive the year. His interview with his son, Paul, which was done circa 1961-62, indicates that he knew he was slowing down.

"I decided to build all the presidents in wood," he told Paul. "So I built all of them up, [but] some of them are not now complete. . . . I didn't get my pictures quite complete. I intended to complete them, [to] make an Indian chief for each president we had in wood . . . . I got my wood, but never have been able to complete them." (The *World* story refers to "some 26 wood portraits of United States presidents – each made with nearly 40 different kinds of wood" on display in the Fiddle House, so Mr. Galloway got reasonably close to finishing the task. At the time, our 35th president, John F. Kennedy, was in the White House.)

"He never did go to the doctor," remembered his neighbor Bobby Holman."If he couldn't doctor himself, well, that was it. The neighbors took care of him when he got sick.

"But he was going downhill. And when he got to feeling bad, he painted that Totem Pole. He said, `I want to get it painted one more time before I die. Nobody else can paint it like me.' He got it all painted, too – built the scaffolds all by himself and put them up there."

Nathan Edward Galloway died on November 29, 1962 and was buried in the Chelsea cemetery next to Villie. As was the case with his wife, his services were held at Chelsea's First Baptist Church and his interment was directed by the Paul Merriott Funeral Home. The *Chelsea Reporter* newspaper summed up Mr. Galloway's influence on the area in an appropriate headline: "Last Funeral Rites for Man Who Brought Many to Chelsea."

In the *Tulsa World* story, which may have been his last major interview, Mr. Galloway appeared to have made provisions for the Totem Pole and Museum to continue after his death. "I'm going to will the land and totem pole to the state," he said. "The wood carvings will go to the Boy Scouts."

These ideas were never implemented, however, and the two decades following his death came very close to bringing an end to his creations as well. Ultimately a story of rebirth and resurrection, the tale of Ed Galloway's Totem Pole Park includes some sad, dark years.

Now, it's time to look at those.

CHAPTER FIVE

Ed Galloway died in 1962. Shortly after his death, thieves kicked down the door of the Fiddle House and stole many of Galloway's fiddles, wood carvings and all of his presidential portraits. Galloway's family moved the remaining woodwork into the home on the property. The home was subsequently ransacked.
– from *Route 66: The Empires of Amusement*

The above statement describes what many people believe happened following Mr. Galloway's death; some say that he didn't even have a lock on the Fiddle House. However, in a *Tulsa World* article published July 12, 1964 – about 20 months after Mr. Galloway's passing, writer Roger Rickard reported a different story:

> His only son, Paul Galloway, 47, of Sand Springs, is working to re-establish most of the works the way his father left them.
>
> A maintenance electrician at Douglas Aircraft Co., Galloway fights a running battle with the elements and the curious to keep his father's works intact.
>
> "As I get around to it, I do a little work; eventually I'll re-establish most of the things the way that he had them," he said.
>
> He removed all of the delicate inlaid pieces, which included 400 hand-made violins, from the "fiddlehouse" more than a year ago because humidity and changing temperatures were ruining them.
>
> "When I get the windows back in the fiddlehouse, fix its floor and get a heating system, I'll move the smaller pieces back in.["]

At that time, the Totem Pole was still attracting plenty of visitors, and no one would've known better than Joe Holman, who, at the age of 32, was still running Little Joe's Grocery next door. He told Rickard that "four or five thousand" had visited the park so far in the year – "But," Rickard wrote, "attendance last year was only half what it was when Galloway was alive, he [Holman] said."

The section of 28A running in front of the Totem Pole was still only gravel then, and Rickard concluded his piece on a hopeful note, writing, "Holman figures the totem's popularity could be restored by fixing up the 'fiddlehouse' and blacktopping the highway in front of the property.

"If Galloway's son maintains his renovation plans and the State Highway Department make a strategic decision, both could become realities."

The Oklahoma Highway Department, in fact, paved Highway 28A in 1965, the year after that story was published. But, ironically, instead of boosting attendance at the park, it apparently provided an escape route for a thief, or thieves.

In 1967, according to the March 19, 1980 *Tulsa Tribune* story by Paul C. Day (which, interestingly, copies the Paul Galloway "As I get around to it . . ." quote from Rickard's *World* story, written 16 years earlier), "most of the fiddles, along with 400 inlaid wood pictures, were stolen. None has ever been recovered."

Regarding the theft, Galloway told Day, ". . . I promised Dad on his deathbed that I wouldn't ever move anything away from the property. I told him, 'Dad, they'll steal us blind.' And he said, 'Son, maybe those folks need these things more than we do.'

"That's the way he was. He was always thinking about the other guy."

However, there were apparently lots of other guys coming through the park during those years who weren't thinking about Mr. Galloway or his legacy – or about much of anything at all besides larceny and malicious mischief. Left wide open and unattended most of the time, with only Joe Holman – and, after his 1968 death, his parents – to keep an unofficial eye on things, the park, Fiddle House, and even Mr. and Mrs. Galloway's now-vacant home were slowly stripped and vandalized by undesirable visitors, often working under cover of night, who carried off just about anything that might hold some value.

Even Little Joe's Grocery was not immune. Following Joe's death at the age of 37 (his tombstone at the Chelsea cemetery reads "[Little] Joe," adding his middle name, Wallace), his mother and father, Earl and Sophie Holman, took over the store. The two ran it for another 21 years, before Mr. Holman's 1989 death, and thievery proved to be a constant problem. "It was open 35 years altogether," noted Joe's brother Bobby. "Before Mom finally shut her down, it'd get robbed every week."

In *Backyard Visionaries,* Barbara Brackman summed up the decline and fall of the park and museum. "Over the years," she wrote, "the park weathered and deteriorated. The paint faded, the weeds grew up around the picnic tables, and the roof of the Fiddle House began to leak."

But even during this agonizingly long nadir of its existence, the Totem Pole still drew visitors and made memories. One of them was Tulsan Steve Jones, who was 17 years old in 1970, when he stopped by the place one Sunday on his way to a ranch owned by some friends in rural Foyil. Along with him was a 15-year-old girl he'd become acquainted with in Tulsa the night before.

"I asked her if she wanted to go out the next day, and she said yes," he recalled in an interview for this book. "So we went to my best friend's ranch in Foyil, where we used to go shoot our guns and have Fourth of July parties.

"I'd always stop at the Totem Pole on the way, and so I said to her, `Let's stop here.' We walked inside the Totem Pole, looked around – I remember there were birds in the top of it – and then I kissed her. It was my first kiss. We were just kids."

At the time of the interview, he and his wife, Pam – the girl he took to the Totem Pole – had been married 44 years, and had moved to Foyil, where they planned to retire. He figured that long-ago smooch inside Foyil's best-known roadside attraction probably had something to do with their move to the area decades later.

"I don't know if there was some fate there or what," he said. "Whatever it was, we're happy."

* * * *

It's a landmark. Something like the pyramids. But there's nothing there, not even a plaque, to tell about it. To me, that's sadder than how rundown it's gotten.
– Totem Pole neighbor Steve Payne, from "N.E. Galloway's One-Man Monument" by John Wooley, *OK Magazine*, February 21, 1982.

And now, please permit the author a personal observation.

In the early '80s, my good friend Ken Jackson, a *Tulsa World* editor at the time, advised me that *OK Magazine*, a Sunday supplement produced by the newspaper, would look at any appropriate stories I might send their way. As someone who had recently abandoned an academic position for the often shaky pursuit of freelance writing, I found this to be welcome news, and set about looking for something to write about.

I found it less than two miles from my home.

Having grown up in Chelsea, I had returned to the area with my new wife in 1979, settling on a small acreage in rural Foyil in what locals called, informally, the Totem Pole Community. So, heeding the old saw that advises people to write about what they know, I headed a mile and a half or so down the road to gather material for a story on Mr. Galloway and his creation.

I spoke to Mr. and Mrs. Holman, still running Joe's Grocery, who both told me about the "dime postcards of the totem pole" that were once hot sellers. And I got quotes from our friends the Paynes, who'd lived in the area for years. As for the Totem Pole, I wrote that it was "now a wind-eroded, graffiti-smeared spectre of former glory that still commands respect and awe."

The story became my first-ever sale to the *Tulsa World*, where I would end up spending 23 years as an entertainment-section writer. And the Sunday morning it was published, as a one-page interior story with two color photos, I drove from my farm-to-market road to Little Joe's Grocery to tell the Holmans it was on the stands.

As it turned out, I could've saved the gas.

When I made the turn on to Highway 28A, I was stunned by the sight of cars parked on the shoulders of both sides of the road. Then, as I got closer, I saw people swarming over the grounds, looking up at the Totem Pole, taking pictures of one another. I found a place to park and went into the store, where Mrs. Holman was busy handing out pop and snacks and even Totem Pole postcards to a crowd of people.

I leaned over the counter and said, "Mrs. Holman, I just came down to tell you that the story was out, but I guess you already know that."

I'd like to think that there was a tear in her eye when she looked at me, but I can't be sure. After all these years, I can't even be confident about what she said to me. But I *believe* I heard her say, "This is just like it was in 1955."

That experience taught me two things. The first was that every public word you utter or write has weight, and so you'd better be very careful with and sure about what you're saying. And the second was that Ed Galloway's Totem Pole and the rest of his creations that still stood in the dilapidated park may have been beaten down by years of vandals and thieves and weather and neglect, but they somehow still lived, and they still had the power to intrigue and attract people.

Certainly, during that dark period in its long history, the Totem Pole was down.

But it was by no means *out*.

CHAPTER SIX

People just tear it apart. They throw rocks at the windows and throw trash on the property. We used to mow and have trash cans there, but we don't get any support in trying to keep it up and we are too old to do it anymore. It is a sad state of affairs.
– Joy Galloway, quoted in "Foyil Landmark May Get Facelift" by Rick Cole, *Tulsa World*, May 19, 1982

The Totem Pole story referenced at the end of the last chapter was published in the *Tulsa World*'s *OK Magazine* on Sunday, February 21, 1982. And while we can only speculate on its role (or lack thereof) in what happened afterwards, by May of that year the Pole had attracted the attention of the Tulsa Historical Society, whose members were considering taking it on as an official project.

As indicated in the above epigraph, it was clear that Paul Galloway and his wife, Joy, were increasingly unable to keep up the battle against vandals, thoughtless visitors, and the elements. As if to put a coda on their uphill struggle, that quote from Mrs. Galloway was published the day after her husband died (although he had of course been alive when writer Cole conducted the interview).

Much of the *World* story was somber, reflecting the frustration of not only Joy Galloway, but also Sophie and Earl Holman, who had their hands so full with running Joe's Grocery "13 hours a day, seven days a week" that they could do little to help the Galloways. The piece ended, however, on a hopeful note.

"THS president Haskell Brady says the society's board of directors will meet next week," Cole wrote, "to consider the possibilities of maintaining the 34-year-old structure." That move, he added, "could pave the way for Oklahoma's biggest totem pole to once again be a major tourist attraction."

It could've. It didn't.

Cole told the subsequent story in the July 14 issue of the *Tulsa World*, which pretty much said it all in the headline: "Totem Pole Restoration Axed." The reason President Brady gave for the THS board turning down the project was a simple one: "We have much to keep up occupied here in Tulsa County and I think it would be best that it be referred to help within Rogers County," he said. "Perhaps the Rogers County Historical Society could be of assistance."

And while the Rogers County Historical Society would, not long afterwards, play a major role in the restoration, things didn't look too promising at the time. Wrote Cole:

> Marleta McGuire, past president of the RCHS, says that the society is quite concerned over the fate of the totem pole, but at this point does not have the funding or the manpower to attempt restoration.
>
> However at its monthly meeting Sunday, the RCHS is going to consider alternatives to aid in the monument's restoration, she said.
>
> "There have been individuals who have, at one time or another, shown interest in the totem pole. Perhaps one of them could be of help," said Ms. McGuire.

As things turned out, however, the initial push to save Ed Galloway's Totem Pole came not from Rogers County, or even from Oklahoma, but from a group out of the college town of Lawrence, Kansas, called the Kansas Grassroots Art Association. In a *Tulsa World* story published November 13, 1983, writer Linda Martin reported that the association had already begun working at the park:

> Saturday [Nov. 12] about 12 members of the group began renovation efforts by putting a temporary plastic roof on the octagonal [Fiddle House] building. Galloway built the structure to house his wood carvings, which included more than 350 violins, most of which have been stolen.

It's the start of "long-term restoration plans," said Barbara Brackman, Kansas Grassroots president. The temporary roof should protect the murals on the interior walls until major repairs can begin.

Calling the Totem Pole and grounds "a gem of `non-traditional' folk art" (as opposed, Martin noted, to "traditional" folk art, which "usually involves single items like paintings or sculptures which can be sold individually"), the writer went on to tell why Barbara Brackman and the other KGAA members had been particularly attracted to Mr. Galloway's 90-foot creation and the "private world" surrounding it:

"Of the 200 to 300 (non-traditional) folk art environments throughout the country, Galloway's efforts resulted in `one of the best,' Ms. Brackman said. 'Mainly because of the design. The guy really was an artist. He had no formal training but his composition, color motifs are really beautiful to look at.'" Paraphrasing Brackman, Martin explained that the KGAA was "an organization of volunteers interested in preserving such environments, which are often destroyed or allowed to deteriorate."

"My mom was really the instigator in getting that property fixed," noted Suzanne Galloway Rogers. "She worked hard on it, and I think she did it for my dad. I really do. Then, the Kansas Grassroots organization came down and worked on it, getting all the right colors and authenticating it to make it look like it had looked before."

Despite having only "about 30 active members" at the time Martin wrote her story, the Kansas Grassroots Art Association ended up sticking with the project for well over a decade, not only laboriously refurbishing what had become the sadly faded and neglected "private world" of its one-of-a-kind creator, but acting as the catalyst for a series of complementary efforts from surrounding communities, organizations, and those who just wanted to help.

JOHN WOOLEY

* * * *

CHELSEA – People interested in contributing to the
preservation of the Totem Pole east of Foyil may make donations to
"Save the Totem Pole" fund at the First National Bank of Chelsea.

The fund will be administered by the Kansas Grassroots Art
Association, a nonprofit organization. The association, along with
concerned Oklahomans, have agreed to a three-step plan to save the
90-foot, concrete totem pole and an adjacent fiddle house.

The association put a temporary roof on the fiddle house in
November to protect the interior murals from further weather
damage. The second step involves hiring consultants in engineering,
historic and paint preservation so as to develop a plan and budget to
preserve the site. The third step will be to raise funds to carry out the
plan.

– unbylined item in the *Tulsa World*, February 12, 1984

It took Mr. Galloway 11 years to build the Totem Pole; it took
even more time than that to restore it. And while the progress may have
seemed glacial to the casual drive-by observer, it was nonetheless
happening. Things were moving forward, and, as the momentum grew,
people around the area started getting involved. One of the first locals,
according to Daris Stimson, was Wanda Rice, owner of Foyil's Top Hat
Dairy Bar.

"I remember Wanda furnished the first breakfasts over there [at
the Totem Pole] to kind of get things kicked off," he said, "to get some
input, you know."

Another Foyil resident, Gerry Payne – who, as a Rogers County
Commissioner, would later make county equipment and manpower
available to Pole restorers – remembered Wanda Rice feeding
complimentary breakfasts to the members of the Kansas Grassroots Art
Association who'd come to work on Mr. Galloway's creations.

58

"They came in a couple of times a year," Payne recalled in an interview for this book, "and they arranged it around their vacations. I think it was around Memorial Day when they tried to do it each year, and then, later on, sometimes in the fall they would get together enough vacation time to come down and work on it."

Both Stimson and Payne, along with wives Sue and Shirley, became charter members of the Foyil Heritage Association, a mid-'80s civic group that grew up around annual autumn events called Foyil Fun Days. "They both started around the same time," said Payne. "They were intertwined, and the Fun Days were successful. So then, they decided to take on the Totem Pole, and raise money for it."

Meanwhile, other fundraising efforts were going on in the area. In the fall of 1984, women of the Chelsea Senior Citizens Center crafted a quilt, featuring, according to an October 2, 1984 *Tulsa World* item, "motifs taken from the designs Galloway incised into the Totem Pole, his Fiddle House and other structures at the handbuilt roadside park." Those interested could buy a chance on the quilt for a dollar, or a pattern to make their own quilt of the same design for $5. Another brief piece from October 31 – this time in the *Tulsa Tribune* – announced that the quilt would be awarded on Saturday, November 3, at Draeger's Shopping Center in Chelsea, with all proceeds going to "the Save the Totem Foundation at the First National Bank of Chelsea."

"The park is deteriorating, and the Kansas Grass Roots Art Association has set up the fund to restore it," noted the unbylined article. "The fund is at $2,966, said Barbara Brackman of the art association, based in Lawrence, Kan."

Fundraising efforts were necessary because government money to fix the Pole and grounds was proving elusive. Linda Martin, in her *World* story, let Brackman explain why.

"One problem in trying to save such artifacts is that they fall through the categorial cracks of governmental funding, she said. `It doesn't fit the guidelines. It's not representative of a specific type of architecture and it's not traditional folk art.'"

So, it was left to the locals and the KGAA to acquire what was needed. And, working together, they did. An April 20, 1986 *World* piece described what was probably a typical joint effort of the time: "Members of the Kansas Grassroots Art Association will join with local volunteers April 26-28 to work on the `Totem Pole,' built by folk artist Ed Galloway in the 1940s and 1950s. The association is a non-profit organization dedicated to the preservation of environments built and designed by untrained artists. Members of the group and volunteers will continue a brush-clearing project and will begin a paint analysis of the Totem Pole for its restoration. . . ."

(According to KGAA president Brackman's chapter in *Backyard Visionaries*, getting the painting of the Pole right was particularly challenging, with the restorers having to make decisions based on photos of and paint chips from the structure. "Because Galloway had painted each piece several times over the years," she wrote, "three or four layers of color were sometimes perceptible, and the chips often conflicted with the photographic evidence." Group members ended up either photographing or making sketches of each piece of the Pole and filling them in with a kind of paint-by-number system based on the 18 different original colors they'd identified from the chips. Those drawings and photos were used as directions for the actual painting of the Pole and other structures at the park.)

Although it's unclear whether the special breakfasts given by the Top Hat Dairy Bar's Wanda Rice were fundraisers or simply a way of helping the KGAA's workers – perhaps they were both – the newly formed Foyil Heritage Association picked up on the idea of feeding people as a way to acquire more money for the restoration efforts.

"It seems to me that the first thing I remember was a fish fry," said Sue Stimson. "[Foyil resident] Fred Keeler helped with that. Then, after that, we started having the barbecues."

Although the annual barbecue dinners, with acoustic musicians from around the area roaming the grounds with their instruments, continue to this day, no one interviewed for this book seemed quite sure when the first one began.

"I'm going to say it was earlier than the '90s," said Daris Stimson. "When we had the first barbecue out there, they [the KGAA members] were already working on it [the Pole], and painting it up so high."

What everyone agrees on is that Trent McSpadden, a Chelsea postman for many years, was, as Daris Stimson noted, "kind of the instigator in that cooking stuff."

Gerry Payne, who often assisted in cooking the traditional beef brisket for the event, agreed. "Trent," he said, "was the chief cook and bottle washer."

Meanwhile, others stepped up to lend a hand in other ways. One of the best-remembered was not a local resident at all, but a retired Dow Chemical employee named Jim Reed, who lived in Tulsa, some 40 miles down Highway 66. A remembrance in the February 2004 *Rogers County Historical Society* newsletter, published after Reed's December 2003 death from a heart attack, outlined his contributions to Totem Pole Park:

> . . . Jim was a tireless RCHS volunteer for over 13 years. Jim drove from his home in Tulsa and volunteered at the Totem Pole Park in Foyil an average of 1-2 days every week during that 13+ year period. Jim was always organizing or working on a project at the Totem Pole Park. He was involved in the organization of or worked on every project at Totem Pole Park since the RCHS acquired it in 1991 and was involved in a few projects there before 1991. Jim cut down dead trees, planted trees, built the Park's 2 picnic shelters, worked on the design and construction of

> the Galloway house exterior, worked on the Fiddle
> house, worked on the play house, brought
> supplies to the park, and worked on Totem Pole
> events. . . .
>
> Jim's drive, boundless energy, and giving
> spirit will be missed. His family asked that
> donations in his memory be made to RCHS's
> Totem Pole Park.

"Jim came in here about, oh, let's say '85," said Daris Stimson. "Somehow, he was just interested in everything around here. I sold him property out there [around Totem Pole Park], and he just picked the ball up and ran with it. He lit the match that got everybody going."

The fiery enthusiasm touched off by Reed continued to burn throughout the late '80s and into the '90s, as members of the RCHS and the Foyil Heritage Association found both big and little ways to collaborate on their shared project.

"The Kansans would come up here on holidays, like Memorial Day or Labor Day," recalled Carolyn Comfort, who became the Rogers County Historical Society's Totem Pole Park director in the early '90s, following the group's acquisition of the area. "The head guy [probably Ray Wilber] had a trailer, a motor home, and he'd bring it and they'd park it out there and cook in his trailer. The Stimsons, I think, loaned them their rest room, and their shower; they did that for several years."

And, as the KGAA members worked on the Totem Pole and Fiddle House, Reed and the Foyil Heritage Association began the restoration of another of Ed Galloway's creations: the rock house he, Villie, and Paul had called home.

"They tore down the old house, right to the foundations and the rock walls," said Gerry Payne. "They left the rock and put a whole new roof up, and windows."

"The windows were a big project," added Comfort. "Do we put in authentic windows, or do we put in windows that keep people warm?

We had a lot of agreements and disagreements about that with the Kansans, because they wanted everything authentic. But when you get authentic, people might freeze to death." She laughed. "We had to do something different about *that*. So the people down in Foyil put in everything that a modern house has – air conditioning, electricity, water – so we could get somebody to live there and watch over the property."

By 1995, the rock house was far enough along for the Foyil Heritage Association to start soliciting donations for its two new doors and 12 new windows. Nearby Adair State Bank paid for the back door, and the RCHS bought the front. The dozen windows were purchased, at a cost of $125 each, by individuals, including Joy Galloway, who'd donated the main part of the park – an acre and a quarter – to the RCHS, which had then turned around and purchased an additional seven and a half acres for an expansion that included planned picnicking and parking areas. Two other windows were bought in memory of a pair of volunteers who'd played significant roles in the rebirth of Ed Galloway's house and grounds: Claremore's Wanda Moore, longtime RCHS president, who'd been in charge in 1991 when the group took over Totem Pole Park, and Bob Bunnell, a Foyil resident and early booster of the restoration efforts.

According to an August 18, 1996 story in the *Claremore Progress*, members of the Rogers County Homebuilders Association also were "instrumental" in the reconstruction of the Galloway home, helping "in both contracting and supplying roles along with many other aspects."

The article noted, simply, "The project is now complete."

Soon afterwards, Lyndon and Lorene Walkingstick became the first tenants of the newly restored home. At this writing, they still live there, with Lorene working four days a week in the Totem Pole Park gift shop and museum.

* * * *

My goodness, I'm so excited these dedicated people are saving his dream.
– Ed Galloway's daughter-in-law, Joy, quoted in "Totem Pole" by Shannon Cavanaugh, *Claremore Progress*, July 1, 1992

For just about a decade and a half, the Kansas Grassroots Art Association had the rebirth of Totem Pole Park at the top of its to-do list. A 1994 copy of the organization's annual report, *KGAA News*, helps convey the extent of the members' involvement. Calling the restoration "one of our most significant projects, and certainly the most labor-intensive," the writer added this:

> Previously, our painting crew used the scaffolding system Galloway designed for himself, but by the time we reached the 30-foot level last fall, it was clear our nerve was not equal to his. This year the County provided us with a hydraulic-lift "cherry-picker" truck that carried two painters aloft. For long days both spring and fall, the patient lift operator deftly ferried the prep crew and painters from owl eye to eagle feather to salmon fin. . . .
>
> While the painters bobbed and daubed, the ground crew tackled the Fiddle House. Volunteers braced and floored the attic, built and painted new window casings, and installed lighting. Materials previously stored on the ground floor were hoisted up into the attic and sorted roughly into shop, house, artifacts, and raw materials. Cleaned and cleared of clutter, with the interior murals exposed and illuminated, the Fiddle House again expresses Galloway's vision . . . .

As the reader may recall, Mr. Galloway, who had all the time in the world to build and paint the Pole, worked outside on pleasant days and found things to do indoors when the weather turned nasty. The KGAA volunteers, however, didn't have that luxury; since they were only able to commit to a few days of labor a year, they ended up working rain or shine.

And sometimes, as Shannon Cavanaugh noted in the 1992 *Claremore Progress* article quoted above, it was all rain.

"'It's rained on us all week. It's been wet and cold,' says [Ray] Wilber as he climbs out of his tent, grabs a bucket of paint, and climbs up the ladder," she wrote, adding later, "Such dedication is why volunteers have finished painting more than half of the Totem Pole park, repaired the museum's [that is, the Fiddle House's] roof, cut all the overgrown weeds and painted all the gate posts."

But even with the volunteer labor from the KGAA as well as from the Rogers County Historical Society and the Foyil Heritage Association, it took money to buy the materials needed. From the beginning, donations and fundraising were essential to the reconstruction and maintenance of the park, and through the years Totem Pole Park boosters employed a variety of methods to keep money coming into their coffers. In addition to the still-extant annual barbecue dinner and the previously mentioned quilt auction (other similarly themed quilts have also been sold or raffled off over the years), a late-'80s, early-'90s promotion offered a certificate for a symbolic square foot of the Totem Pole in return for a donation.

Then, in 1995, one of Mr. Galloway's fiddles was put up for a drawing. (Although many had been stolen from the Fiddle House during the days following Mr. Galloway's death – and never recovered – his family still had some in storage.) A brochure from the Rogers County Historical Society, asking "Would You Like to Own an Original Ed Galloway Fiddle?" described the instrument, which would go to the holder of a five-dollar donor card:

> Mr. Galloway created many fiddles from exotic woods. This one is primarily of myrtle wood with the likeness of an Indian carved on the scroll. It is number 162, signed by Mr. Galloway

and dated 1956. This is the only one he made of myrtle and is the only one that has been offered to the public. W.L. Rhode, noted violin maker in Tulsa, added the finishing touches, stringing the bridge and the bow.

In 1997, the RCHS and Foyil Historical Society began another fundraiser, which also continues to this day. At the time, Jim Reed had designed and installed what RCHS called "a commemorative circle" at the base of the Totem Pole Park flagpole. For $30. interested parties could buy one of the bricks in that circle and have it inscribed with up to 42 characters. Since then, dozens of people – including famed Route 66 author and *Cars* star Michael Wallis – have had their names inscribed on the bricks, providing an ongoing source of revenue for the park, and a source of remembrance for those so honored.

CHAPTER SEVEN

It's a constant process – kind of like your home. You're always working on it.
– Carolyn Comfort, quoted in "Long-time volunteer promotes unique Rogers County Attraction" by Rebecca Hattaway, *Claremore Progress*, August 21, 2005

In 1991, retired educator Dr. Carolyn Comfort moved with her husband from Tulsa to Claremore, where she found herself living across the street from Rogers County Historical Society president Wanda Moore. At the time, the Comforts had a son attending the University of Kansas in Lawrence – which also happened to be the home of the Kansas Grassroots Art Association.

"He kept saying, `How come you never say anything about the Totem Pole Park?'" she recalled in an interview for this book. "I'd tell him, `I've never seen the Totem Pole Park.' And he'd say, 'Well, mother, there *is* one. There has to be. People from Lawrence work on it.'

"Where I made my mistake was asking Wanda where the Totem Pole Park was," she added with a laugh. "So she took me out there, and that's how I got involved in it."

The same year Comfort became involved with RCHS and its Totem Pole project, Joy Galloway donated the heart of the park to the group, which in turn bought several acres around it for future expansion.

"She did wonders," said Suzanne Galloway Rogers of Carolyn Comfort's subsequent work at the park. "I have to give her a lot of credit."

In 1993, Comfort took over as RCHS's director of the project (a year before Wanda Moore's death); by that time, she'd become well acquainted with her counterpart from the Foyil Heritage Association, Jim Reed.

"I was the Rogers County Historical Society's chairperson on Totem Pole Park for 16 years," she said. "Jim Reed and I worked together for probably 10 of those years, and then he died."

Those years, ending with Reed's passing in 2003, were productive ones for the Pole and its environs. As Daris Stimson noted, "Carolyn and Jim made a pretty good pair."

"She was about like Jim," added Sue Stimson. "She was the one who kept us going."

Both Reed and Comfort – as well as the Stimsons and many others involved in the refurbishing – were on hand for the celebration of a milestone on June 15, 1996, when the Galloways' renovated rock home was first opened to the public. A program for the event features two columns full of the names of in-kind contributors; the facing page lists the window and door purchasers and another 18 individuals and companies that pitched in with "Materials, Money, Discounts & Installation" – showing how widespread the interest was in the home rebuilding, as well as in the park itself.

As we saw in the last chapter, however, the house wouldn't be completely finished for a couple more months. So Carolyn Comfort did a bit of improvisation.

"I took some of my furniture and put it in the house so it would look like it had been lived in," she remembered. "I talked somebody into fixing draperies for us, and so it looked really good. We must've charged a little bit for people to come into the house, because it seems like we made some money off of that."

The next year, deeming the restoration efforts on the Pole and the Fiddle House complete, the members of the Kansas Grassroots Art Association – whose invaluable participation had begun nearly 15 years earlier – packed up their tools and paintbrushes and returned home for good.

But, as Comfort noted in the epigraph at the beginning of this chapter, there was always more to be done. The 2005 *Claremore Progress* story that quoted her listed some of the post-1997 highlights:

> . . . A 16-foot carved and painted wooden pole was added to the top of the totem pole in 1998. In 1999, the park was added to the National Register of historic places.
>
> More recently, promotional videos have been made and Boy Scouts have developed a nature trail on the property. . . .
>
> Two more racks of fiddles made by Galloway are now on display in the "Fiddle House" museum and gift shop, bringing the total number of fiddles to 135.
>
> Galloway's daughter-in-law, Joy, donated the additional fiddles that had been in storage since the 1960s.
>
> "They were full of wasps' nests and had to be cleaned up and refinished," a project Comfort's husband and grandson took on, she said.

The Boy Scouts' nature trail, running a half-mile through four and a half acres of woodland surrounding the park, began in 2001 as an Eagle Scout project for Casey Garrett and Jared Marsh, members of Claremore's Troop 23. With the guidance of the Rogers County Historical Society, Garrett staked out the trail, while Marsh built a footbridge over the little creek that ran through the area. Other Troop 23 members aided in the effort, with Jesse Emanuel building the bench and the sign at the entrance, and Brandon Warfield covering the trail with gravel.

Ed Galloway, of course, had spent much of his life working with boys at the Sand Springs Home, and he must've been particularly fond of the Scouts. In George Kane's 1962 *Tulsa World* interview, Mr. Galloway told the writer, "I'm going to will the land and totem pole to the state. The wood carvings will go to the Boy Scouts."

While the disposition of Mr. Galloway's estate didn't work out that way, the fact that Boy Scouts have been involved with his park — and his legacy — would undoubtedly be a source of pride to him. As Carolyn Comfort told the Claremore Progress for a January 5, 2003 story, "Involvement of Boy Scouts was a dream long ago of Ed Galloway."

* * * *

We went out there to Totem Pole Park this last fall. I'd been there one other time, but that was before anything had been restored, and it was all grown up in weeds and the fiddles were knocked out of the Fiddle House. So it was really great to see that they were working on restoring it all, and they had a bunch of the fiddles that he'd made, and some of the furniture he'd made. I thought that was really nice. The grounds were all mowed and kept. It looked *completely* different from the time I'd seen it before, probably in the mid-'70s.
— Mr. Galloway's third cousin Robert Gideon, in an interview for this book

While other improvements have come along in the succeeding years, including the installation of a septic system and public rest rooms for visitors, the resurrection of Ed Galloway's Totem Pole Park was essentially completed in 1997. It has stood proudly as a major roadside attraction ever since, even as big changes happened all around it. In addition to the Kansas Grassroots Art Association leaving, following the completion of its work on the Pole and Fiddle House, the Foyil Heritage Association disbanded in April 2006 — bestowing the money it had on hand to the Rogers County Historical Society, "with the stipulation," noted Sue Stimson, "that it go in the Totem Pole fund."

Two years later, in June 2008, Joy Wofford Galloway died and was buried next to her husband at the Fair View Cemetery in nearby Talala.

Then, in 2010, Carolyn Comfort — who'd become known around the area as "the Totem Pole guru" — stepped down from her long-held position with RCHS and turned the job over to David and Patsy Carmack Anderson. Unlike Comfort, who'd never laid eyes on the Totem Pole until Wanda Moore took her to see it, both David and Patsy had grown up around it.

"It was something to be proud of," David said. "Any time we had company, we'd always take them and show them the Totem Pole. I remember one time we went into what's now called the Fiddle House, and I met Mr. Galloway. He showed me the fiddles that he worked on. Just a really nice fellow."

"I remember going up and going through the Fiddle House; that was the main thing," added Patsy. "The door was always open, and anytime you went to the grocery store, you could go through there."

Living on a farm road a little under three miles from the Totem Pole, a teenaged Patsy made regular trips to Little Joe's Grocery, where Joe Holman was still the proprietor.

"I didn't have my [driver's] license, so I couldn't drive to Chelsea and grab stuff at the store," she said with a laugh, "but I could drive to Joe's."

Following their graduation from Chelsea High School, the Andersons got married and left the area, with David's job as a soil scientist for the USDA taking them to Colorado and elsewhere. In 2007, following his retirement, they moved back to Rogers County, to a home and ranch only a couple of miles from Totem Pole Park. Three years later, they became its co-directors, still under the auspices of the Rogers County Historical Society.

The reason the Andersons became involved in the first place has to do with an area artist named Virginia Krugloff, who spent a lot of her time during the year 2009 repainting the Totem Pole. Working through the Rogers County Historical Society, which had received a $3,500 grant from the international historical-preservation group the Questers, she often found herself braving hostile elements to get the job done.

"Virginia had three scaffolds, and that wasn't high enough, so she put a ladder on top," recalled museum employee Cilla Wolfe. "The wind would blow so hard that she'd put her arm inside the ladder to hold the paint can and stay up there all day, painting like that."

It's little wonder that the artist sounded proud of her efforts in an interview with *Tulsa World* reporter David Harper for a story published Dec. 7, 2009.

"Krogloff of Claremore, who specializes in restoration projects, said that initially she was just going to oversee the effort," Harper wrote. "However, the self-described perfectionist ended up basically doing it as a solo project.

"'I got it done my way,' she said."

It was while she was doing it that she attracted the attention of David Anderson, who happened to be driving by one day.

"I saw her on the ladder on top of scaffolding, and I told her I'd be interested in helping do the painting," he said. "She gave Carolyn Comfort my phone number, and she contacted me about becoming the director."

"If they hadn't met," added Comfort with a laugh, "I would *never* have gotten out of it."

In addition to making sure Ed Galloway's Totem Pole Park is properly maintained and the gift shop inside the Fiddle House stocked, both David and Patsy Anderson continue to plan for the future. At the time of this writing, they were seeking funds to repaint the figures at the top of the Pole. (In the *World* story, Krugloff notes that "the top half of the totem pole still could use some more work.")

"And if we have any money left," David said, "I'd like to build a bigger pavilion."

There's another thing he'd like to do, too, although he's not at all sure it'll ever happen.

"I have always wanted to climb up to the top of that thing," he said, grinning. "We've been directors now for four years, and I have yet to do that. I'm not sure I trust those old ladders. I doubt if any of them are Mr. Galloway's, but I know there are ladders in there from when they did the restoration, back in the 1990s."

If he does make that trek, he added, he'll have to have something else on hand.

"An EMT," he said with a laugh. "I want one in the immediate vicinity."

ABOUT THE AUTHOR

John Wooley is a writer and radio host who has written, co-written, or edited more than 30 books, including *Shot in Oklahoma*, a look at Sooner State-lensed pictures that was named Best Book on Oklahoma History for 2011 by the Oklahoma Historical Society. In addition, he served as guest curator for an Oklahoma History Center exhibit, *Oklahoma@ the Movies*.

He has also written a number of documentaries, including the Learning Channel special *Hauntings across America* and, in 2014, *Oklahoma Military Academy: The West Point of the Southwest*. He also scripted the made-for-TV feature *Dan Turner — Hollywood Detective*, starring Marc Singer, Tracy Scoggins, and Arte Johnson.

An entertainment writer for the *Tulsa World* newspaper for 23 years, Wooley has seen his freelance articles and interviews appear in a wide range of publications, from *TV Guide* to the horror-movie magazine *Fangoria.* He currently hosts the public-radio series *Swing on This* and serves as a contributing editor and columnist for *Oklahoma Magazine*. His writing has earned him induction into the Oklahoma Music Hall of Fame, the Oklahoma Jazz Hall of Fame, and the Oklahoma Cartoonists Hall of Fame.

Made in the USA
Columbia, SC
12 June 2017